S

STAYING POWER

Reflections on Gender, Justice, and Compassion

Carter Heyward

The Pilgrim Press

Cleveland, Ohio

The Pilgrim Press, Cleveland, Ohio 44115
© 1995 by Carter Heyward

"The Power Within Us" copyright 1990 Christian Century Foundation.
Reprinted by permission from the March 14, 1990 issue of *The Christian
Century*. "Staying Power" from *The Witness* 77, nos. 1–2 (Jan./Feb. 1994):
6; "The Bear and Bosnia" from *The Witness* 76, no. 10 (Oct. 1993): 8–10
(amended version). Reprinted by permission of *The Witness*, 1249
Washington Blvd., Ste. 3115, Detroit, Mich. 48226–1868.

00 99 98 97 96 95   5 4 3 2 1

Library of Congress Cataloging-in-Publication Data
Heyward, Carter.
     Staying power : reflections on gender, justice, and compassion /
Carter Heyward.
         p.   cm.
     Includes bibliographical references and index.
     ISBN 0-8298-1027-7
     1. Feminist theology.   2. Homosexuality—Religious aspects—
Christianity.   3. Christianity and justice.   I. Title.
BT83.55.H49   1995
230'.082—dc20
                                                         94-39963
                                                            CIP

With gratitude and love,
and in memory of
my best friend when we were little girls,
Elliott Streetman Hubert
(1946–1994),
I dedicate this book to
Angela,
Bob DeWitt,
Jim Lassen-Willems,
and
Jan Surrey

spiritual companions
political inspirations
beloved friends

CONTENTS

Preface: Re-Imagining Justice

This book is a resource for the struggle in hard times, the struggle for justice.

In theology, as elsewhere in life, we depend on the power of language to draw sisters and brothers into understanding with us the experiences, commitments, questions, and meanings that are most important to us, the things that generate our passion. With this book, as in much of my work, I am interested in calling especially, though not exclusively, white liberal and radical christian women beyond our attachments to the individualistic "self" concept of a liberal religious and political epistemology—how we learn about and know ourselves, one another, the world, and God.

The re-imagining of language is something feminist and liberation theologians have been doing for some time now. There is nothing new about such a cultural project. Yet it seems to me more critical than ever that folks who honestly desire a more just and compassionate world be clear *with one another* how we do, and do not, envision the justice and compassion that we seek. Only insofar as we are clear in this way, thereby allowing differences with our friends to emerge, publicly and unapologetically, can we stay in the struggle *together*, holding and working out our differences relationally,

in community, over time; in faith that what we cannot resolve will be taken up in new ways by those who come after us.

I am especially concerned today that many white feminist
women, like our white male allies, have become so attached
to the liberal notion of the individual "self"—self-growth,
personal recovery, and the psychologizing of all our pain and
trouble—that we are giving up our sacred power to participate in changing the world: not just our own personal world
or the social world in which we're most comfortable with
those who think like us and act like us and understand us, but
the *whole* world of many cultures, colors, beliefs, complexities, and contradictions. How do we "stay" with this real
world teeming with violence and pain? How do we embody
together the power to stay with the struggle, not letting go of
our personal needs for growth and recovery—which are important and not to be trivialized—but rather grounding our
needs and well-being in the struggle for justice and compassion?

We move toward understanding this world and our "staying power" as we begin to shed the liberal concept of
"justice" as the outcome of a system of litigation by which
fairness actually can be achieved. This concept of justice pre-
supposes that the playing field is level and that all persons
begin the race at the same place. It is a colorblind and gender-
blind ideal that has little to do with reality.

Breaking with the liberal justice tradition that sees no differences among us, I think we must insist that justice cannot
be achieved unless we take our differences seriously. Where
our differences are acknowledged and understood in terms of
their cultural, political, and economic meanings, justice making is a radically relational *movement* and an ongoing *process* of
creating, struggling for, and envisioning right relation
among us. In addition to its legal, political, economic, educational, and psychological dimensions, justice making has

spiritual roots and blossoms that this volume explores. In right relation, the integrity of each group, person, or creature is respected and, if possible, preserved. Integrity is itself a relational quality, not an individual's "possession." To have integrity is to be struggling for right relation. Right relation is not violent or indifferent. It is not patronizing or condescending. It is not created by professionalism, law, or coercion. Right relation requires, and generates, mutuality as its basis—a way of being in relation that presumes our radical interconnectedness as sisters and brothers. Politically and professionally, as well as in the smaller realms of our personal loves and friendships, mutuality is seasoned through shared authenticity. A genuinely right relationship seeks not to be exploitative because it is committed to the integrity of all participants. If abuse or harm occurs in a relationship in which persons are struggling for mutuality, amends should be made and efforts taken, if possible, to restore the integrity of those involved.

Most persons and creatures have been so distorted by fear, rage, and hatred that we do not often live rightly with others except in frayed and tattered ways. Still, most of us yearn for right relation and have glimpsed it in those moments when justice *has* rolled down like waters, when love *has* conquered fear, when politically powerful people *have* forgiven their enemies, when women *have* been able to escape from the violence of their abusers. When we are making and embracing right relation, or catching it in glimpses, a power working through us is enabling us to connect in mutually empowering ways—a power calling us more fully into who we are, collectively and individually, when we are rightly related.

This power to create justice, to make right relation, to sustain mutuality, and to make amends where we fail is sacred power. It is the power of God, *ours* insofar as we share in it. We do not god alone. We bear sacred power in our connectedness with the whole creation. In this sense, both theologically and ethically, we literally are involved in one another's lives. *Theologically*, we are *already* mutually related simply because we are here in the universe, sisters and brothers, friends in the Spirit. *Ethically and pastorally*, we need to help one another learn how we actually can embody this friendship, how we can construct our societies and institutions, our work and relationships, our values and spiritualities in compassionate ways that contribute to our shared and individual capacities to live rightly together.

Our compassion—literally, our capacity to bear with one another's lives and suffering—is the deep psychospiritual recognition that we *are* friends, brothers and sisters together in life, whether or not we like it. Compassion is the wellspring of a nonviolent commitment not to harm one another, even our enemies, if we possibly can help it. Compassion invites us genuinely to repent wherever we have brought harm and to allow others to do the same.

These theological themes run through these chapters. I can write about these spirited blessings, of course, with a great deal more ease than I can live them! One of the most important lessons I have been learning slowly during my almost fifty years on this planet is to accept my own ragged edges and simply let myself be, a day at a time.

My thanks to Richard Brown, editor of The Pilgrim Press, for supporting this project; to Pat Hawkins and Jeffrey Mills for pooling their splendid editorial and secretarial skills in helping prepare the book for publication; and to Joan Sakalas and Jane Hicks for assisting with research and indexing.

Finally, so much gratitude to Bev Harrison and Peggy Hanley-Hackenbruck, without whom in either case my life would not have been filled to this point with such love and joy as well as sadness. Your inspiration marks these pages.

PART 1

Mutuality

Rather than finding a place to stand in history that is somehow "ours," a moment in which we are comfortable and from which we draw spiritual strength through memory or nostalgia or repudiation, we need to help one another find ways to move and bend and change together.

1

Not Knowing for Sure

As I reflect on the call of Matthias, the thirteenth man tapped to be part of Jesus' migrant band of disruptive voices, I find myself thinking about what the Lenten season might teach us about who we[1] are and what we're here to do, wherever we may go in the world, helping lead the way, not because we know so well how to do it or where we're going but simply because the lot has fallen upon us. We are, in the words of the fourth gospel, "friends" of Jesus, not his "servants," but his friends.

Several weeks ago, I was quoted in the *Boston Globe* as speaking for the faculty of the Episcopal Divinity School.[2] The words from my mouth, words spoken by me but in a different context, conveyed the image of both a woman and a school that are arrogant—a charge we do hear from numbers of our critics. This image, striking hard yet again at the heart of what we here mean to be about, left me pondering our christian[3] vocation, corporately as a school as well as mine personally, as one theologian and teacher. Questions of arrogance and humility have accompanied me into this Lenten season as a focus of prayer and reflection.

With these questions and this homily in mind, I was touched by the account in yesterday's news of Justice Harry

Blackmun's "renunciation" of the death penalty.

Most of us will not be able to record our theological, ethical, or political changes on the front page of the *New York Times* like Justice Blackmun,[4] the eighty-five-year-old senior member of the U.S. Supreme Court, but we perhaps can take a lesson from this old man who wrote a passionate, solitary dissent from the Court's upholding of the death penalty in the case of a Texas inmate.

"From this day forward, I no longer shall tinker with the machinery of death," he wrote.

> For more than 20 years, I have endeavored—indeed, I have struggled, along with a majority of this Court to develop . . . rules that would lend more than the mere appearance of fairness to the death penalty. . . . Rather than continue to coddle the Court's delusion that . . . fairness has been achieved . . . , I feel morally and intellectually obligated simply to concede that the death penalty experiment has failed . . . I am . . . optimistic . . . that this Court eventually will conclude that the . . . death penalty must be abandoned altogether. I may not live to see that day, but I have faith that eventually it will arrive. The path the Court has chosen lessens us all. I dissent.[5]

My desire is not to romanticize old age, which is seldom kind, especially in a culture that so fears and tries to avoid it, but rather to lift up the gift that the justice is offering those who have ears to hear: *humility*. Being able to admit failure. Confess mistakes. Lose. Dissent from an immensely popular opinion. When senior sisters and brothers bare their souls and tell us that they've been on the wrong side of an important struggle, we do well to listen. Because they're offering us a gift, and it has not come cheaply, and there is likely some deep wisdom in it.

Of course, the temptation for most liberals in hearing Blackmun's words is to be pleased that he has learned what many of us have believed all along—that the death penalty is morally wrong because it cannot be administered fairly in an unjust society. I was pleased that Harry Blackmun has concluded that state-sponsored murder is wrong. But the lesson this story signals for me is less directly about the death penalty than about what it may signal to us about arrogance and humility (hence also, perhaps, about the death penalty).

Unlike his younger colleague Antonin Scalia, Blackmun has consistently seemed to me a bearer of *humility*. I don't mean self-effacement but rather that he is standing with common people. Blackmun seems grounded in an assumption that he is connected with the rest of humankind. In this spirit of what makes us most fully human, most fully sisters and brothers together, the senior Justice has struggled to interpret the law in ways that respect not some but *all* of us in our common needs for survival resources, including opportunities for education, work, and procreative options.

Whatever else we are called to, you and I, as those upon whom the lot has fallen, we are called to humility—to experience ourselves as sisters, brothers, and friends—born into the world to *share* it. Unwilling to uphold the systems and structures that do, in fact, divide us, setting humans over other creatures and the creation itself, male over female, white over black and brown and yellow, richer over poorer, christian over pagan, those in this historical moment who call themselves "heterosexual" over those who have been branded and differentiated—that is, set outside the christian cultural norm—as "homosexual" or "bisexual."

It is important that those of us in the christian church be clear that our strong emphasis on *justice*—sexual and gender and racial and economic justice—is rooted in a commitment to struggle for right relation, not to divide and separate women from men, gay from straight, white from other colors, or middle class from poorer or richer people. The fact is, our christian body, and the body of creation itself, is fragmented, splintered, terribly, horribly divided. This is our context, the actual situation in which our vocation is to help find, and help lead, the way toward the healing and liberation of our body, as christians, as humans, and as God's creatures who share the earth. We cannot help lead unless we are able and willing to see and hear and speak truth as best we can, including the horrendous truths of the violence and injustices that threaten to undo us all.

Yes, together and individually we are called, like Justice Blackmun, to ministries of "renunciation" and, also like this man, to vocations of "annunciation," which is the other lens through which all christians seriously interested in justice and compassion must view our lives and work: renouncing structures and institutions that breed injustice and evil and, at the same time, announcing the coming of the Spirit into our lives, bringing liberation where there is despair, healing where there is brokenness, life where there is death.

So how do we do this, how do we bring life, healing, and liberation? How do we embody and share this passionate spiritual and political work as christians without being arrogant about our lives and work, individually and collectively? Put positively, how do we live and work in the spirit of humility which is the life-bearing spirit of God that brings healing where there is woundedness, liberation where there is bondage? How does humility work?

We would do well to help move one another beyond popular christian notions about humility which are really not so much about humility as about *appearing* to be closer to God than others—being self-effacing, thinking of others rather than self, having no pride in self. These notions of humility, well-cultivated in advanced monopoly capitalism as a spiritual remedy for self-absorption, may at times function to soothe our consciences, but they contribute little to the ongoing creation, liberation, or blessing of the world.

In fact these pious, arrogant notions of the humble man or

woman who seeks nothing for him or herself but all for the glory of God are steeped in theologies that serve neither the spirit of life nor the people and creatures of God very well, because they presume the separation of God from the world and of one creature from another. These theologies presume that if I am for myself, I cannot be for you; that if we are for ourselves, we cannot be for others; and that if we are for one another, as human and creaturely sisters and brothers, we cannot be for God. To the contrary, the only way we can be for God is to be for one another and for ourselves in right relation with one another. The only way we can live humbly with our God is to live rightly with one another.

Humility, then, is being in right relation, friends—connected at the root of who we are—bearers of sacred spirit with and for one another. All of us have more to learn than to teach about who we are as brothers and sisters, abundant and resplendent and mutually respectful in our differences; earth creatures, with a great deal in common, beginning with our common needs to love and be loved in ways that enable us to grow, and learn, and thrive.

How then may we know the difference in this spiritual work between arrogance and humility, ours and that of others? There are, I believe, several clues.

First, humility is radically relational. It is born in a right, mutually empowering relation, which invariably and always is the work of justice making with compassion. Humility is a desire that the other's well-being and our own be held and cultivated together. In this way, the spirit of humility seeks out those whose voices are not being heard, those whose well-being may be overlooked, those whose language may not be understood. If a sign of humility is an open hand, arrogance could be imaged as arms crossed securely over one's chest as if to say, "I've got it. I've got whatever I need." Arrogance is founded in self-containment and self-possession, of disconnection from our commonness.

There come magical moments in our lives, the Olympics calls this to mind, when we stand out individually, in Whitney Houston's lyrics, have our "one moment in time."[6] It is, of course, not arrogant for a Bonnie Blair, a Johann Olav Koss, or a Kim Ki Hoon[7] to experience ecstasy at their extraordinary accomplishments; we love it and it is wonderful. But for any person or nation to assume sole possession of the Gold, or the God, or the Way, exclusively and forever, epitomizes an arrogance that, on a larger historical and political stage, is fascism—more closely at home for most of us, "the American Way" running amok.

Second, as a relational way, humility is dialogical. Humble folks both state their claim and invite response, dialogue, and mutual transformation—not simply conversation between two parties who have their minds already made up but intellectual and moral wrestling in which everyone has something to learn and teach. *Humility is seasoned in the spiritual and intellectual work of genuine dialogue.* Arrogance is often veiled: I say that it's "God's" will or "the tradition" or "the church's teachings" or "for the good of others" rather than something I myself need, want, fear, or hope for. So, while arrogance may or may not state its claim, it does not genuinely invite dialogue. It cannot, because it cannot be moved. Arrogance, by definition, is mightily resistant to change.

Third, humility involves struggling and changing. While arrogance is characterized by unchanging systems, minds, and ways of being in the world, humility involves changing in relation—changing our minds, as Justice Blackmun has; changing our lives; admitting wrongdoings; making amends; tolerating, even at times celebrating, the ambiguities of our lives as fertile spiritual soil. Being humble means struggling to know and do what's right. Arrogance need not struggle, but rather is intent upon upholding the good and the right, without question or dispute.

Fourth, humility allows us to be more genuinely present with one another, professionally as well as in other ways. I want to say a good bit about this, especially as it pertains to our work as pastors and healers. We need, I believe, to be developing some "professional humility," which is becoming more and more difficult for some complex reasons.

In their commitment to end sexual exploitation, many feminist professionals, whether or not they intend this, are lending uncritical support to traditionally structured dyadic relationships between a (usually male) expert and a less knowledgeable, less powerful, and/or less healthy (often female) person.[8] The distorted shape of this relationship does nothing whatsoever to promote the well-being or liberation of women of any culture or class and much to secure our subordination and oppression. This quintessential professional relationship transparently reflects, and supports, white western men's assumption that an unchanging power-over relationship is the optimal resource for psychospiritual and physical healing. This arrogance, I submit, is the root of sexual and other forms of professional exploitation.[9]

We cannot stop sexual exploitation by tightening up professional containers that are themselves exploitative. We need rather to be rethinking, re-imagining, and working together to transform the professions. I believe that a goodly portion of christian vocation is the re-imagining of ministry, lay and ordained, and of working together to uproot structures of sexual, physical, economic, and psychospiritual abuse. In our re-imagining, we need to consider the likelihood that "professionalism" itself is the institutionalization of white middle- and upper-middle strata economic control in a historical moment in which we and our world are out of control—economically, sexually, and otherwise—and in which we are scared.

Rather than deal honestly with our fears and one another, we become increasingly "professional." The churches, of course, should be helping us deal more honestly with our fears and one another. But this would require among clergy and lay leaders the humility to let go of our desire to be professionally distant from those with whom we work, who thereby are "safe" from us (just as we are from them). This professionalism is inhibiting us from being honest with ourselves and others in our work. In this context, the helping professions are less and less likely to help people cultivate many truly sustainable resources for personal healing or social liberation.

I see this as basically a problem of our having too little professional humility—too little mutuality, dialogue, willingness to struggle and change. We need some humility, which we can only cultivate in community, "professionals" and "nonprofessionals" alike being honest with one another about our fears and hopes and faith and doubt. If we were to loosen up the professional constraints so as to allow us to conspire—breathe together—a little more freely, we might find ourselves and others becoming more fully human to one another, able to discover how to be nonexploitative in our communities and relationships, how to be more genuinely moral persons in community.

Finally, humility doesn't know for sure. If, in arrogance, we are closed off to the new or different, then, in humility, we are a little more open to the possibility that we don't know exactly what we're doing—and this means all of us. I, Carter Heyward, don't know for sure, and never will, and you can quote me. Only with others, including those whose opinions are different, can I/we come to know what we need to know and do at this time. And our knowledge will always be limited—yours, mine, and ours. We will never know for sure, and yet we are not reduced to silence and passivity.

How then do we, as activists, writers, teachers, pastors, speakers, hold such uncertainty? How do we live and work together, never knowing the future of our churches, our schools, our workplaces, our communities, our lives as individuals? Does this lack of certainty not move us more fully into the heart of *faith*—into an openness to what we do not know on the basis of what we believe about ourselves, the world, and God? Does it not require "revolutionary patience,"[10] not with injustice or oppression, but with ourselves and others as we learn, and relearn, and learn again, how to make right relation in the larger and smaller places of our life together?

Harry Blackmun doesn't know for sure that the death penalty is wrong, any more than he knew for sure in 1973 that for the state to allow safe, legal abortions for women was right. Death penalty and abortion debates are fundamentally *moral* discourses and they always will be, regardless of the politics and economics that shape them from one period to another. *In the moral realm, we will never know for sure.* We can only do the best we can, and then only with one another's support and patience. That's what ethics should be all about, helping us live as responsibly and compassionately as we can with ambiguity and uncertainty. Beyond that, we can only turn ourselves over to the sacred spirit that is shaping us as fully as we will allow.

Can we accept gratefully the critical challenge being put to us: to help shape the church's morality—not only its sexual and gender morality but its social conscience and relational compassion? Our lives, if we are listening to one another, will move us into and beyond controversial questions about sex and gender and we will begin to see together, in our racial, ethnic, class, and cultural differences, that these "sexy" issues are controversial precisely because they have so much to do with how we and others understand ourselves, the world, and God.

May we live, here and wherever we are led, in a spirit of humility, open to complexities we cannot fully comprehend and uncertainties we cannot control.

2

Staying Power

I'm one of those almost-fifty-something people who are grateful for the 1960s. I'm thankful my spirituality, my experience and understanding of the world and God, has some tenacious roots in that period. I'm grateful for what the 60s taught me and lots of other folks about values and priorities and dreaming *big* dreams.

Three decades later some folks, including lots of "60s people," deride that moment in our recent past as a poignant one of dreams that either could never have been realized ("the age of Aquarius") or already have (as if racism were a thing of the past). This repudiation is either a dismissal of the power of a dream or the failure to make connections between what was achieved during that turbulent decade and what was not. For people who lived during this period or who have met it mainly through media and oral tradition to disavow the 60s as hopelessly idealistic and culturally chaotic or as a long-ago time which is no longer ours is to turn away from a wellspring of our most sacred power to participate in shaping our own historical moment.

For history is a movement, not a collage of separate pieces that can be judged apart from one another. Like Rosa Parks and Martin King and Malcolm X, we,[1] too, are dynamic or-

ganisms whose lives cannot be either lived fruitfully or as-
sessed fairly apart from the broader sweep of history and the
communities of sisters and brothers who came before us,
who will come after us, and who are with us now. The
meanings of the 60s do not lie behind us but rather are ours to
create, for the value of a historical moment is not inherent,
self-evident, or static. We are creating the meaning of the 60s
in the relation between then and now, them and us, ourselves
and our forebears and our children.

Rather than finding a place to stand in history that is
somehow "ours," a moment in which we are comfortable
and from which we draw our spiritual strength through
memory, or nostalgia, or repudiation, we need to help one
another find ways to move and bend and change together.
This is the church's spiritual work, our ethical foundation as
christians. We need to be learning, theologically, to experience time itself as movement in the life of all that is human,
creaturely, and divine, forever changing and always in relation to whatever has been already and whatever will be.

In the movement of God, the 60s are not over and done,
and they never will be. We who are here now, in this moment, are creating the pastoral and prophetic significance of
that decade by how we are living our lives right now. We today are responsible for whether the 60s will be remembered
largely as a decade of cynicism, violence, and pipedreams or
as the sacred moment of a dream of justice that was and still is
possible.

But to keep the dream alive, we, like Martin Luther King,
must let it grow and change and become whatever it needs to
become to include the well-being of those whom we didn't
remember in the 60s—women and children of all colors and
cultures; gay, lesbian, bisexual, and transgendered people;
disabled people; the earth and its many creatures; Hispanic
peoples, Native peoples, Asian Americans, Jews, Palestin-
ians, most poor people, and the many, many others left out

of a struggle waged primarily in black and white.

Thanks to the prophetic King and others, with him, whose vision widened during the decade of Vietnam, the 60s brought many progressive christians toward the brink of recognizing the spiritual bankruptcy of advanced capitalism. For the next thirty years, our political economy would advance globally. Purely for profit, it would be tightening up *economic* structures of racial, sexual, and class exploitation that most white middle-strata liberals had barely noticed during the 60s.

And this brings us to the 90s, in which every ethical issue in our life together—in the United States and throughout the world, from healthcare to sexual violence to rainforests to children dying of hunger—is defined politically and addressed economically primarily in terms of how it upholds or threatens the advancement of global capitalism. What in this world are we christians to do about this treachery? What *can* we do in the 90s?

If the 60s are alive in us as an inspiration, then we progressive christians are being called to dream and to let our dreams grow bigger and to make no peace with those who would thwart the dreams of a world in which *all* God's people and other creatures are sisters, brothers, friends in the sacred Spirit that is our power to keep on keepin' on. We should remember, however, that we, too, are failing to see clearly who is being left out in this moment.

May we learn more and more how to live and work, struggle and celebrate, in an openness to all that we cannot see.

3

The Power of God-with-Us
Theological Lessons from the 1980s

The year 1980 saw the dawn of *Nicaragua libre* and the impending U.S. presidency of Reagan, its ardent foe. This was a period in which the pernicious AIDS virus was moving among us, and we were unaware. It was three years before the invasion of Grenada and six before the falls of Marcos and Duvalier. It was a time immediately before the emergence of *glasnost* and of Gorbachev. It was just before the beginning of death-dealing cutbacks in already small measures of care for people of color, women, children, other marginalized persons, as well as animals, plants, and minerals of many sorts. We were on the verge of a high-tech boom that would threaten further to diminish our senses of ourselves as co-subjects in the sensual work and play of creation. In this context, I was studying black, feminist, and Latin American liberation theologies and was becoming convinced that a justice-making church could make a difference in the world.

A dissertation on a "theology of mutual relation" would, ironically, provide my fare into the security of a profession not well known for the mutuality of its practices or its theories. But, at age thirty-five, I would be officially out of school for the first time in thirty years, and I leaped into the decade with a blessing in my pocket worth more than the

Ph.D.—unbounded enthusiasm for the theological vocation. Amid ups and downs, delights and sufferings, deaths and births, burnout and rekindling, I have been carried by the past decade more fully into an appreciation of honest theological work. I have been learning to recognize it, at its root, as a spiritual passion that we need in the world and that the world needs in us.

Let me back up a little. While a graduate student, full- or part-time, at Union Seminary in New York for over a decade, I had been working in the city, in parishes, hospitals, and shelters, learning as much about human life as about its divine source and resource.

I remember sitting under a tree in the summer of 1980 with United Methodist minister Michael Collins (who later would die of AIDS) and several other members of the minuscule gay-lesbian caucus of the Theologies in the Americas "Detroit II" conference. We spoke of how grateful we were to be learning with our theological "elders" that the sacred spirit of life can be experienced as the power moving us in the making of justice with compassion.

I was sure that sooner or later the church would get it. Surely the liberal christian communities would come to see the rightness of the theologies of liberation that were being generated globally by christians and others struggling for bread and dignity. The basis of my optimism was, I believe, no facile "liberalism." In the company of discerning teachers and learners, my education was being shaped out of certain assumptions that had as much to do with living life as with thinking about it: that we are "in relation" whatever we may think of that fact, that the most basic human unit is not therefore "the self" but rather "the relation," and that this intrinsic mutuality demands—and should be the foundation of—our ethics, politics, pastoral care, and theologies.

Drawing on the existential theology and social philosophy of Martin Buber, I wrote in my thesis that God is our "power in relation" and that justice, the actualization of love among us, is the making of right, or mutual, relation. Without realizing it I was trying to articulate a relational *ontology* as a companion piece to the profoundly *moral* motives and commitments of liberation theology.

My graduate studies had sparked my interest in human life as a relational matrix in which God is born. (The coming decade would stretch my imagination toward an intense interest in the connectedness of all life.) I felt a certain euphoria upon graduation. Happily donning a yellow button on my academic gown that read "Better Gay than Grumpy," I stepped into the 80s and the ranks of professional theology as an active, indignant, and optimistic teacher and priest with a ragged-edged commitment to justice for all oppressed people.

The 1980s brought me to some new places—more exactly, I suppose, into new ways of standing in old commitments and values. It is not simply that my mind changed. My mind —how I think theologically—would have had to have been put on ice not to have been changed in some degree of conformity with its relational matrix.

Maybe as it grays, every theological generation loses some of its youthful idealism. But if, in changing (as we must to stay well), we do not hold stubbornly to the roots of this idealism, we will be sucked into a funnel through which our theological vision will narrow and, in time, become rigid and false. I am disappointed in my generational peers who look back upon "the 60s" with patronizing scorn, as if we ought to be a little embarrassed for having dreamed those dreams. I am learning that I do not trust those whose dreams become less daring with time.

I am not as busy as I was in 1980. There's still much to do and I may be better able to do some of it, but I am doing less. I am not as optimistic as I was that organized religion will make much headway in creating a more just and compassionate world. I now understand better the conservative character and structure of the church, having been working within it (or at its edges) as a priest since 1974. I am less idealistic. I do not expect that many who hold authority in the church or other dominant institutions of our lives will be converted, en masse or as individuals, to the serious work of justice making with compassion and good humor as their top priority. But I'm not cynical. My faith in the power of God-with-us—our creative, liberating power with one another—is secure and my hope for the world is being radicalized. My companions in living, working, and visioning, the claims of justice, and the urgings of the spirit are pushing me closer to the roots of the idealism and enthusiasm I embraced ten years ago. I am beginning to imagine the implications of the connectedness of all life, my own and that of other humans and creatures. I see more completely the importance of living in such a way as to celebrate the struggle for mutuality (the actual dynamic of justice making) not only as an ethical ideal but as the very essence of who we are in the world—the basis of our survival. I am learning that, in this ontological and ethical sense, our we-ness literally creates my I-ness and that this is a very great good. It is the foundation of what it means to be human, what it means to be "in the image of God."[1]

My learning has been partially the result of a *via negativa*, recognition of not only the absence of mutuality and justice but an active opposition to it in the doctrines of selfishness and domination incarnate during the 1980s. I am at least as indignant today as ever and no less hesitant to say so. I am angry that a culture of alienation and despair, of greed and violence, is being constructed for profit on the bodies of the poor, the elderly, the young, women, blacks, browns, gays, lesbians, and other people and is being masked as "kindliness" and "gentleness" by those who have learned to believe their own lies. Beverly Harrison, a beloved friend and companion for almost thirty years, reminds me of "the power of anger in the work of love."[2]

If good humor is, at heart, a sense of perspective, I think I am maintaining it by *enjoying* being alive in the world. I delight in my friends, my students, my niece and nephew, movies and music, my animal companions, and a little land and home on the Maine coast. I love walking and dancing and singing and laughing.

Still, I suspect that those who do not care for pushy broads, feminist priests, happy dykes and faggots, and irreverent references to the god of heterosexist, racist patriarchy are likely to find me every bit as ornery as before. Recent years have dipped me into the wisdom of sages like feminist poet Judith McDaniel who warn that trying to be "nice" on terms set by those who hold the power in place is to "sell ourselves short."[3]

Specifically, then, what am I learning? *I am learning that, without some serenity, I could not continue in the struggle for justice.* Like that of many U.S. citizens visiting in Nicaragua during the 80s, my time there, in 1983 and 1984, was an unexpected blessing. I did not go seeking a gift. I went to be educated and to show solidarity with those struggling against the contras. In fact, my traveling companions and I were given a glimpse into the life of a people fighting enormous odds for the chance to live together in a just and peaceful society. Scores of Nicaraguan christians and others met us with what seemed unflappable confidence in themselves and in their spiritual or moral vocation to struggle for justice.

Not until I had been back in the United States for several months did it dawn on me that I had experienced a profound sense of serenity in these people and, through them, had glimpsed my own confidence and inner strength, elusive through much of my life as a white christian in the United States.

I have wondered why so many white people learned in Nicaragua during the 1980s what we well might have learned here at home—in active, ongoing solidarity with, for example, black sisters and brothers or Native Americans. Was it easier to go to a faraway land to see what has been happening right before our eyes? Easier because it felt safer, less intimate, or because we did not know how significantly our lives would be touched until it was too late to stop the transformation?

Nicaragua shook my foundations. As the experience grew in me, I found my commitments stronger than ever and, at the same time, I felt depleted and depressed. I was enraged about U.S. imperialism; hurt and angry about how women and gay and lesbian people are treated everywhere, especially in the church; horrified by the blatantly racist practices of the Reagan administration; immensely saddened by the death of my father in 1984; frightened by a breast cancer scare a year later; working too hard in a seminary that drains its feminist professors to meet the demands of increasing numbers of women students; and just plain tired.

It took me several years to see that, in the early 1980s, my faith was in serious crisis. As I left for Nicaragua, I was burning out. Had I ever, really, believed in resurrection? Had it occurred to me, deep in my soul, that *resurrection is a relational movement,* the revolutionary carrying-on of a spirit of love and justice that does not and will not die? Had I ever truly believed that the Spirit needs us to do her work in the world, to move as slowly as we must in order to build this world together as a common home? Had I really seen that we are never called to come forth alone but always to answer the Spirit's call *with* one another, drawing for strength and wisdom from what womanist theologian Delores Williams has called our "lines of continuity"?[4]

This trust in the foundations of one's life has roots in the experience of right, mutual relationship. Thus at the core of our faith we know that, in the beginning and in the end, we are not alone. In our living and in our dying, we are not separate from one another. Reminiscent of Jesus, Martin Luther King, Jr., and others who have seen this, Archbishop Oscar Romero prophetically voiced this confidence when he promised, "If they kill me, I will rise again in the Salvadorean people. . . . My hope is that my blood will be like a seed of liberty."

In the strength of such faith, an inner peace can begin to form. Perhaps this incipient confidence enabled me in 1985 to speak to a friend, a former student, about my drinking problem and to hear his response: "It troubles me that someone who teaches and writes so much about mutuality is so resistant to seeing that you need help with this. You can't stop drinking alone. Why don't you take your own theology seriously?" An epiphany, this encounter.

The next morning, with another friend, I attended my first meeting with other alcoholics and began recovering, one day at a time. In the spirit of the Nicaragua pilgrimage, this process is continuing to open me to the real presence of others and myself to them, opening us to the power released among us in a vulnerability that, because it is authentic, common, and shared, is sacred.

I don't believe any more now than before that we must participate in organized religion to be involved in the work of justice. But I know today that we[5] need shared senses of spiritual or moral bases upon which to build our lives and commitments.

I am learning the critical necessity of approaching our theological work the same way we do any authentic spirituality: through the particularities of our lives-in-relation. A hermeneutic of particularity involves studying the ways in which our differences contribute to how we experience and think about human and divine life.

In a racist society, a black god/ess is not at all the same as a white god/ess. In a hetero/sexist situation, a goddess is different from a god. In a sex-negative culture, an erotically empowering spirit is utterly distinct from an asexual and erotophobic god who needs no friends.

Through the work primarily of feminist christians, I have been led to Sophia/Wisdom,[6] to "Christa/community,"[7] to Hagar the slave woman,[8] to Jephthah's daughter[9] and those who fight back on her behalf: images that are redemptive *because* they are dark, images of black or marginalized women, vilified, trivialized, rejected, silenced—and resisting their oppression and that of their sisters. As our historical imaginations unfold, we may begin to recognize in these images a call to struggle against injustice and to celebrate our woman-lives.

A goddess whose tender, outraged presence heals and strengthens abused women is entirely different from the God in whose name troubled fathers and priests sometimes rape girls and boys. I have been taught this less by my feminist professional colleagues than by my students who are also in treatment for wounds inflicted by men (and sometimes women) who abused them as children or as adults. Their stories often suggest the appalling extent to which the church tends, not simply to ignore sexual, physical, emotional, and spiritual violence against women and children as a major crisis, but actually to provide theological justification for this violence in its teachings about male headship, women's subordination, and the sinful character of sexuality. The sex-as-sin obsession which characterizes christianity has produced a repressive, guilt-inducing sexual ethic which, in turn, generates a pornographic culture of eruptive sexual violence.

I am learning that I cannot teach christian theology constructively unless I am aware that, historically, the church has done much to damage women, Jews, Muslims, people of color, and the whole inhabited earth and unless, as a christian, I recognize how our doctrine, discipline, and worship continue to reflect and contribute to this abuse of power.

I became clearer during the violent decade of the 1980s that it matters a great deal what god-images we use in our worship. I am becoming increasingly resistant to participating in, much less leading, liturgy from which dark, erotically empowering, woman-loving images of God are absent or concealed. The consecration in 1989 of Barbara Harris as an Episcopal bishop signaled hope for many of us. This was not because either the Episcopal church or one powerful, capable woman, black and beautiful and prophetic, can move mountains. It was rather because the choosing of such a bishop by the Republican-Party-at-prayer conveyed the kind of lovely, unexpected contradiction that christians love to call "paradox." Bishop Harris is a living, breathing reminder that just about anything can happen when two or three are gathered in the spirit of justice.

During the 1980s, my understanding of God was, in the spirit of Mary Daly, "gyn/ecologized."[10] I believe that God is indeed our power in mutual relation.[11] I see more vividly than before that our redemption requires that this power come to us, and through us, in healing and liberation, advocacy and friendship, love and sisterliness, in the most badly broken and frightening places of our life together and as individuals. In a racist, heterosexist, class-injured world, God is likely to meet us often in images associated with children, poor women, black, brown, yellow, and red women, lesbian women, battered women, bleeding women, and women learning to fight back. Dark images. Like Mary's poor little boy, God is seldom welcome in reputable places. The story is not a nice one. Good theology is not respectable.

I am learning that, as a process of liberation from either injustice or despair, healing is a process of finding—if need be, creating— redemption in suffering. The AIDS crisis has been teaching me this, as did my father's nine-year bout with cancer, which resulted in his death. More recently, the sickness and death of a

young friend and a devastating relational rupture that left me
badly hurt and in need of healing have required me to struggle with the meaning of suffering.[12]

As we live in the 1990s with an economic structure that
is killing poor people, a movement against crime that is in
fact a racist assault on the urban poor, an unapologetic "post-
feminist" contempt for women and girls, and a mounting
ecological crisis, we will need as much as ever to be able to
create liberation in the midst of suffering.

I have never believed in "redemptive suffering" as a means
of justifying either pain or God.[13] I still do not. There is no
theological excuse for the pain inflicted upon human and
other creatures by human beings. There is no justification, no
spiritual reason, why forces of nature such as hurricanes and
viruses hurt us or why some of us get hit by cars or lost when
planes crash. The death of my life-loving father was not
good, nor was the death of my friend Dianna, nor the agony
of her spouse and family. From a theological perspective,
whether pastoral or ethical, suffering is not good for us.

Although the sacred Spirit in no way "wills" or sets us up
for suffering, all living creatures do suffer. In these last years,
scarred by AIDS, by the dominant culture of greed and violence, and by personal loss and pain, I have come to see more
distinctly the vital link between the healing process (traditionally the prerogative of religious and medical traditions)
and the work of liberation (assumed to be the business of revolutionary movements for justice).

The link is in the commitment of those who suffer and of
those in solidarity with them to make no peace with whatever injustice or abuse is causing or contributing to their suffering *and* in their commitment to celebrate the goodness and
power in our relationships with one another—especially, in
these moments, with those who suffer. To struggle against
the conditions that make for or exacerbate suffering and to do
so with compassion—"suffering with" one another—is how

we find redemption in suffering. To realize the sacred power in our relationships with one another and to contend against the forces that threaten to damage and destroy us is to bear luminous witness to the goodness and power of God. In the midst of suffering, we weave our redemption out of solidarity and compassion, struggle and hope. In this way, we participate in the redemption of God.

PART 2

Healing

So many of us have been so badly wounded by forces of homophobia, misogyny, racist fears and hatred, class injury, and other forms of violence and abuse. But to be blessed by God—and this blessing draws us as close as we will ever get to the heart of God—is, in the beginning and the end, to be empowered in our woundedness, not "in and of ourselves" and not "by ourselves," but with one another's solidarity. To be blessed by God is to become bearers together of the passion and grace of one who liberates us from violence and oppression precisely by joining us in it.

4

Immersed in God's Passion
The Blessing That Will Not Be Taken Away

On the evening of July 28, 1974, Daniel Corrigan, a retired, justice-loving bishop of the Episcopal Church, spoke quietly to the eleven women who were to be ordained priests the next morning in a controversial service that would be declared "invalid" several weeks later by the Episcopal House of Bishops.

Anticipating the trouble that lay ahead, Bishop Corrigan furrowed his gray brow and warned us that, because our ordination was taking place without the church's authorization of the ordination of women priests, many Episcopalians would probably consider it null and void. Not only was it likely that our ordination would be rejected by the Episcopal church as premature and unacceptable at this time but we eleven might *never* be accepted as priests—long after women's ordination was accepted. We would be stigmatized as pushy broads, troublemakers, which, of course, we were. It was our call, our role, at the time. We were ready to accept the stigma for a while, but could we live with it forever? Could we begin to comprehend it as a dimension of God's blessing upon our lives?

What I remember most vividly from Bishop Corrigan's meeting with us was his startling proclamation that we were already priests. "You must never forget it," he smiled as he nodded. "You are priests already. You will always be priests. No one can take this away from you."

This was a stunning assurance with profound theological, political, and pastoral roots and implications. If the wise old man was right, we would not be marching into the sanctuary the next morning to receive a new blessing but rather to confirm something that had been given already. As Alice Walker suggests, we would not be going to church to find God but rather to share God.[1] Already touched and strengthened, we would be going to celebrate God's blessing.

So also today. We[2] gather to celebrate a blessing already bestowed which draws us together from many places. A blessing upon which we come to dwell for a moment in this festive spirit. A blessing which most surely is changing our lives just as it is the world and church that are our home. But we must be clear: to be blessed by God is a dangerous thing. It is in the very nature of blessing—of being touched by the power of love, strengthened by the wellspring of justice— that those who have the audacity to seek divine blessing, even to wrestle with angels and demand it, must take the consequences.

I am speaking of what it may mean to be blessed by God, because we have been blessed abundantly: The Holy One who breathes our only hope into the world; She whose tenderness and tenacity topples principalities and powers; He whose compassion and humor fortifies our lives one day at a time; this God has gathered us to celebrate a blessing we have been given, each of us in his or her own way—and yet, it is a common blessing, something we share, and therein is its sacred power.

Like Jacob, none of us individually earns this blessing. God does not touch and strengthen people because of merit. In fact, you may recall from Sunday School that this Jacob who demanded and received God's blessing was a real horse's ass—deceptive, scheming, manipulative, and, of course, sexist (which doesn't count much against him in christian and Jewish scripture, since nearly all holy men are). Except, arguably, for his attitude toward women, Jacob would not have been the sort of character that synagogues or churches would likely seek to commission as a leader.

Even in relation to his patriarchal God, Jacob was a defiant upstart. Case in point: God comes to Jacob in the form of a man, and they wrestle all night. In this moment, Jacob is the strong contender, though the man manages to dislodge Jacob's hip in the course of the struggle. (As I read this passage a number of times, I found myself thinking that a less erotophobic religious tradition would have plenty of creative erotic interpretations of this transparently sensual story about close physical intimacy, struggle, and love between two men.) As the night wears on, the man says to Jacob, "Let me go, for the day is breaking." But Jacob says, "I will not let you go unless you bless me." Now my hunch is that neither Jacob nor anyone else who insists upon God's blessing has much sense of what they may be in for if they get it.

But you and I have been struggling, many of us for a long time, wrestling for blessings with angels whose power often brings us to our knees; at least as often, I hope, to our feet; and, eventually, to our senses.

Coming out is, for many of us, an ongoing process of wrestling with the sacred spirit. Similarly, getting sober or abstinent can involve fierce contention with God. Seeking ordination or making any vocational pilgrimage can pull us into what may feel like an abyss of struggle with all manner and means of divine and human spirits. Becoming increasingly attentive—politically, spiritually, psychologically, and otherwise—requires serious wrestling with angels. This involves getting rooted in mutual relation in all arenas of our lives—in our work as well as our love. It requires a commitment to make connections between how we love and how we work, our lives and those of others, our well-being and that of others, the injustices done to us and by us and those done to others, by others.

We have done some wrestling, all of us, or we wouldn't be here today. And here we are to name and celebrate the blessing for which we have struggled: this "new thing" that God is doing, somehow through us and with us, because we have had the tenacity to hang on to our hope for the world in the context of a church that ostensibly offers us very little hope. And we have had the audacity to hang on to our hope for the church even as the spirit has warned us that our lives would be easier, safer, less confusing, and quite acceptable to God (as to most of our brothers and sisters) if we were to lower our expectations of how fully human or divine our life together on earth ought to be shared and celebrated.

To refuse to let go of a God who has instructed us to do so? To intrude into a healing session by raising the roof, pushing our way into the presence of the healer Jesus? The spirit of justice seems to require friends and lovers whose audacity and tenacity, even in the face of God, is formidable and, probably, to most religious and other leaders, embarrassing; folks insistent upon God's blessing; folks who won't take "no" for an answer.

So, what is this blessing we so stubbornly have sought?

It is an awakening of our *passion*, our capacity to "bear up" one another's lives in the fullness of who we are together, an ability to experience the real presence of God here on earth in active engagement with one another, our brothers and sisters, and all creatures great and small.

God has blessed us with this passion, this capacity to participate in whatever is most real, most authentic, in our daily lives and in the life of the Spirit. We are given an ability not to view the world, ourselves, others, or God through "rose-colored lens," not to deny our real feelings in our living or our working, not to turn away from involvement in the suffering of the earth and its many varied creatures.

In truth, this blessing requires us to *suffer with* others—not because suffering is good for anyone, but because we cannot love well unless we are willing to bear with one another in suffering and to work with one another toward the elimination of the conditions and forces that contribute to violence, oppression, and injustice. This *compassion* is the essence of the love of God that is with us here and now.

Blessed with such passion and compassion, we cannot be indifferent to what our nation, in our greed and fear and ignorance, has done throughout the world to other nations, peoples, and creatures. We cannot close our eyes to the injustices nourished during the 1980s by Reagan-Bush, which continue to take virulent forms of racism, hetero/sexism, economic exploitation, able-bodyism, and religious and cultural imperialism at home and abroad. We cannot avoid making these connections. We cannot avoid personal involvement in the AIDS crisis—not only as people with AIDS and their friends, families, and colleagues, but also as their religious, ethical, and political allies and advocates.

Blessed with passion, we are opened to our erotic power as the sacred power which reflects our deep yearnings to connect in mutually empowering ways. And this, for lesbians and gay men, may be the most particular, poignant, and compelling dimension of God's blessing that we are here to celebrate.

Because the dominant culture is so bound up in fear—especially a fear of erotic power as sacred, mutual, and creative—lesbians and gay men have become scapegoats of the larger society's inability to deal honestly with sexuality. This means that we carry around lots of projections of other folks' sexual fantasies and sexual fears. In a nutshell, *their* erotic power gets trivialized or twisted and they see it, name it, and punish it as *ours*.

In this badly distorted sexual context, we lesbians, gay

men, and bisexual sisters and brothers have both an enormously difficult and an immensely critical opportunity to be opened more fully to celebrating our erotic power as sacred, our erotic power as the love of God which touches and strengthens us, making us proud and public and happy! *To bear this unapologetic, sex-affirming witness is, I believe, the special, luminous vocation of lesbian and gay leaders in the christian church today.*

The blessing we are given, this passionate opportunity to live life fully, means, of course, that we live in tensions from which there is no escape—no therapy, no Twelve Step Program, no prayer, no person, place, or project can eliminate the tension in a life being fully lived between experiences of anger and compassion, grief and joy, confusion and clarity, fear and confidence, powerlessness and power. To live in such tension is to live in reality. Normally, it is to be "in touch," to live as well and healthy people.

And so, God's blessing to us is not only the passion which roots us in tension and, at times, contradiction; it is also the *grace* by which we are able to bear the tension with a goodly amount of serenity, humor, and gratitude, one day at a time.

I have an old dog, named Teraph, whom I got at a shelter as a gift to myself in 1976 when the Episcopal Church authorized the ordination of women. This wonderful old beast is, in some ways, my oldest soul mate. He is certainly among my most beloved friends and companions. I am finding it hard to watch the life draining slowly out of him as he goes, gradually and steadily, blind, deaf, lame, incontinent, confused. I sit beside him a lot nowadays and stroke him and weep. But I also snuggle with him, laugh, and reminisce in his presence about our earlier days together, what he was like as a pup, what *I* was like. . . . From the beginning, Teraph has been a source of gratitude and, increasingly, serenity in my life. As we have aged together, he has shown me how to slow down. He has helped me learn to feel the depths and heights and in-betweens. He has brought me much delight and joy and, now, as he goes, he is bringing me sorrow—but he is also comforting me in it. From Teraph, I am learning a great deal about the grace of God.

Unless we are able to realize the grace of God as it comes to us through friendship, pets, and nature, through prayer and solitude, through solidarity with others in suffering and struggle, through lovemaking, music, play, and meaningful work, we are likely to burn out, give up, or go mad. For, having wrestled with angels, we will be left exhausted in the midst of ongoing tensions and, often, in the context of sorrows too deep for words.

We are living with AIDS, rejected by those we love, losing so much. And the worlds around us and within us fester with sores of abuse and betrayal, hunger and grief, addiction and violence, confusion and fear. Sometimes it seems that our most frequent visitor is despair, who comes knocking daily on the door. Sometimes it feels like we have been left comfortless by the spirit with whom we have struggled, left to bear alone what, alone, is *unbearable* pain and sorrow.

To be blessed by God is to be drawn deeply into understanding the motive and urgency of the psalmist's cry: "How long, O God?" and Jesus' cry: "My God, my God, why have you forsaken me?"

It may help us to remember that part of Jacob's blessing was a dislocated hip—a wound to remind him, perhaps, not only of his human limits but also that God had indeed been with him. God had, in fact, touched and blessed him. The presence of God had not been merely a dream!

But the blessing we are here to name and celebrate is finally more than simply the passion to live a fully human life, more even than the grace to live it with serenity, humility, and humor.

What Jacob did not know when he demanded God's blessing, what the paralytic did not realize when he was lowered through the roof in pursuit of Jesus' healing power, what few among us today seem genuinely to take in is that *God blesses us by joining us.* The power of God touches and strengthens us by becoming our power in right relation. To be blessed by God is to be drawn into the very essence of the sacred, involved intimately with the Holy Spirit in the work and play of creation and liberation—and to become bearers ourselves of blessing.

From a christian perspective, it is to become *christic*[3] participants in a movement in history that carries us into the fullness of a shared humanity and, thereby, into the fullness of a shared divinity. From a christian perspective, we become active, passionate, erotically empowered and empowering members of the "Body of Christ."

No longer do we simply wrestle with angels, though we may well continue to do this forever. Nor shall we go on forever raising roofs or defying ecclesiastical authorities in order to get into the liberating presence of God, though perhaps we shall have to do this many times as well.

Blessed by God, we ourselves become resources of God's blessing. Healed and forgiven, we take on the work of healing, liberation, and forgiveness. We become those to whom men, women, children, and other creatures come seeking God's blessing.

This may be terribly hard for many lesbians and gay men to imagine: ourselves as bearers of God's passion, God's grace, and God's transforming presence, not only to one another but to the rest of the world—and to the church. It may be hard for us because so many of us have been so badly wounded by forces of homophobia, misogyny, racist fears and hatred, class injury, and other forms of violence and abuse. But to be blessed by God—and this blessing draws us as close as we will ever get to the heart of God—is, in the beginning and in the end, to be empowered in our woundedness, not "in and of ourselves" and not "by ourselves," but with one another's solidarity. To be blessed by God is to become bearers together of the passion and grace of one who liberates us from violence and oppression precisely by joining us in it. God transforms reality by being involved in it—and so, too, do we who are blessed by God. We share the sacred power to create, liberate, and bless the world because we are drawn *by* this power into the suffering of the world, to participate in its transformation.

To embody this transforming power together, to celebrate and share it in our work and play and prayer and passion for justice, to touch it together through our lovemaking and friendships—this is not merely to *experience* the love and power of God, it is to *reveal* it—to make it manifest—to become a living epiphany ourselves!

And so we need not fear the spiritual power of bishops or other adjudicatories, those who hold authority over us in the church and elsewhere in the world. Those who preside over the mainline churches today are, on the whole, out of touch not only with what is happening among erotically empowered and empowering gay men and lesbians in the church but also with what is happening among most folks who struggle for sexual, gender, racial, economic, and other forms of justice in the world and church. Most of these prelates, administrators, and others with ecclesiastic authority, like their secular counterparts, are confused and frightened people who do indeed have the authority to badly damage us and others. For that reason, we must resist the violence and abuse they have set in motion and usually fail even to notice. But we need not fear their power to break or diminish the spirit among us. They have no power to do so.

As these men and women are ready, they will come—if not to us personally, they or those who come after them will come to our nieces and nephews, our sons and daughters, those who will inherit this work from us. We can be confident, they will come, and we will be ready for them. For the lines of continuity that connect us, generation to generation, are sturdy, expansive, and welcoming. They will come, these bishops and pastors, these priests and doctors, these teachers of good order and institutional etiquette will come to wrestle with us. They will come, lowered down through roofs, seeking forgiveness, healing, and liberation.

May we realize that God's blessing upon us—that for which we have wrestled, some of us for so long and so fiercely—is that we be empowered to welcome and bless those who, like Jacob, indeed like most of us, do not deserve to be blessed.

May we sustain the confidence and courage, the compassion and humor, to realize the sacred power in this stunning opportunity which is ours today and will be ours forever.

This blessing will not be taken from us.

5

Fleeting Moments of Safe Space

Many folks today are interested in finding some "safe space." We[1] hear this plea for safety and we make it ourselves, those of us who've been wounded, victims of one abuse or another, which is most of us here and probably all. But what space actually is safe in this world and does the fear that leads us to the demand for safety not stand in some tension with the Spirit poured out upon women and men who will "see visions," "dream dreams," and "prophesy"?

Last week I returned to the Carolinas for my mother's birthday celebration. My family spent several days at the beach, taking long walks, together and alone. On one of those walks, my sister Ann and I reminisced about how, despite parental admonitions about such dangers as getting drowned in the ocean if we went too far out, we'd grown up fairly oblivious to danger in the world. Our parents wanted mightily to raise us in safety, to protect us from forces they themselves didn't always understand.

It was not that we weren't being affected by such menacing forces as white race supremacy, male gender superiority, and an economic order inflicting deep psychic wounds on us. These threats were shaping us, but we didn't notice them, those of us who had either the privileges or the denial systems, or both, set in place to block our vision. We didn't see that there was any ongoing, constant danger—and certainly not that we were in it. We knew there might be an occasional bad person to come along, but in our minds and experiences these people clearly were the exceptions. We did not expect bad things to happen.

Theologically, we had an up-beat view of human nature and a benign, appreciative view of God. We pictured an old, white gentleman who treated everybody, good and bad alike, with kindness. Not until I became a professional theologian did I realize what an Anglican I'd become at my mother's knee!

As we walked, my sister and I simultaneously thought of a prayer we'd learned as girls and we began to say it out loud:

> O God, in the quiet of the morning hour,
> give me the wisdom, patience, power
> to view the world today through love-filled eyes,
> to be gentle, understanding, wise,
> to look beyond what seems to be
> and know thy children as thou knowest them.
> And so, *naught but the good in anyone behold*,
> Make deaf mine ears to slander that is told.
> Silence my lips in all that is unkind,
> May only thoughts that bless dwell in my mind.
> Make me so loving be, *so full of cheer*,
> that all I meet may feel thy presence near.
> Clothe me with thy beauty, this I pray,
> help me reveal thee, Lord, throughout this day.
> —Origin unknown (emphasis added)

I'd learned this prayer in 1957, when I was twelve, at a girl's camp in the mountains of North Carolina. I was so taken with it that I taught it to my five-year-old sister Ann who memorized it and several years later put it on a poster, circled it with dried flowers, framed it, and gave it to our mother for her forty-eighth birthday. To this day it hangs on Mama's wall in Charlotte.

Ann and I agreed that the prayer reflects theology with which we can still live, with a few changes. She reminded me that, even at age ten, she'd rejected this business about being "full of cheer," so much that she'd left it out of the gift for our mother.

I said that one of my most difficult psychospiritual passages has been learning, over time, to recognize evil and the danger in which we live and breathe. I said I would no longer consider praying for a distorted capacity to see nothing but the good in others or in myself in relation to others. In the global societal realms, as well as in intimate relationships, I've had to learn to see beyond the good in persons into the evil that we do to one another. I grew up not expecting to be hurt or to hurt others. It has become clear to me that this failure to see the emotional and physical danger, the political and economic danger, the racial and sexual danger, and the spiritual danger is a failure born partially of privilege but also of a denial of pain by people who want to see ourselves as "making it."

I believe that one reason some of us in theological education are scorned by so many church leaders is that we here are trying to take seriously the fact that there are forces in the world and church that are "not healthy for children and other living things." We notice, moreover, that these forces have been sanctified historically by the church. I'm thinking of racism, of sexism and heterosexism, of advanced monopoly capitalism, of imperialism, and, of course, in these days, of militarism as well. I'm thinking of hierarchical power arrangements established as givens within government, business, and the professions: power over dynamics of control codified theologically as the essence of christian doctrine, discipline, and worship, both catholic and protestant. We are being called to prepare folks for pastoral and prophetic work in the context of a dangerous world that, in many ways, has been created and blessed by the church itself. We are being called to see the good in one another, to love this good, and to see beyond it to the harm that is being done to, and by, us. We are being called to see the evil as well as the good and to learn how to love one another with ever-deepening compassion. This is what we are here at seminaries and in the world to do.

So then, in this context, is our spiritual mandate as a people to create safe space for one another? There are, I believe, two right answers to this question—of course, and certainly not. (And we need to do a power analysis to see why both answers are right, and necessary.)

Insofar as we take the victim of any abuse seriously, our immediate agenda as, or on behalf of, the victim will be to create safe space. There are any number of ways in which safety is created for people in danger: the Underground Railroad, the Sanctuary movement, mothers' flights to protect their children from their fathers' sexual or physical exploitation, shelters for battered women, homeless people, runaway kids, homes and hospices for people with AIDS, refugee work, emergency work in the wake of war, typhoons, famine, any disaster. Of course, we must create safe space which, at its best, is communal space shared by those who do not deny the pain or the wrong that has been done and who know that safe space, if it is good space, will always be empowering.

The creation of safe space, however, is not an adequate ethical response to the problems of violence and danger in which we live. Surely Jesus, Peter, and the others would have loved some safe space for themselves and others. But this was exactly what they could not find as long as they were standing with those in danger, challenging structures of abusive power both within and beyond their religious institutions. There is little safe space for those empowering others to pick up their beds and walk toward liberation, healing, and safety.

There are only *moments* of safe space in the struggle for justice—no permanent place of safety.

This brings us to a paradox in all healing and liberation: seeking to find safe space for others as well as ourselves, we find ourselves in danger. In this sense, our vocation can never be simply to create safety but rather to take the risks involved in standing with those in danger, thereby putting ourselves in danger as well. Central to this spirituality is not an "ethic of safety" but rather what feminist theologian Sharon Welch has named an "ethic of risk,"[2] which is an ethic of radical love.

My nephew Robert has a "zoo book" that tells how lions get their prey: they roar—and the poor victim is literally frightened stiff. Unable to move, petrified by fear, it becomes the lion's dinner. An ethic of safety doesn't enable us to respond creatively to the lion's roar. When we are naive, in full denial, we either don't see the lion or we don't believe it will hurt us. We assume the world is, or can be, a safe place for everyone if only we individually can learn kindness, serenity, and morality. We do not see the structures of evil, the massive, dangerous impediments to this learning. An ethic of safety steeped in denial and naivete is a quintessentially liberal ethic that works best for folks with a goodly amount of race, class, and/or sex privilege.

When, on the other hand, fear has us in its grip, like the lion's prey, we can't budge. In the face of real danger, we become rigid. Incapable of moving, we literally are set in place and devoured by that which we most fear. Our fear becomes our undoing and this can be as great a danger among us as any form of violence or abuse will ever be. H. Richard Niebuhr is remembered as having said, "We watch what we fear, and we imitate what we watch."[3]

The lion is roaring today! And in the face of this very real danger, certain cultural phenomena are emerging—notably, a proliferation of twelve-step programs modeled after Alcoholics Anonymous; the institution of psychotherapy as a popular commodity among the middle class; and a movement of childhood sexual abuse survivors. As someone in recovery myself, I'm no stranger to either the need for healing or the attempts of therapists and twelve-step programs to respond to this need. The twelve-step program has been an especially remarkable source of healing and empowerment in my life, and I'm deeply grateful for it. But I want to signal a warning: like *all* spiritual and psychological resources, the twelve-step programs, psychotherapy, spiritual direction, the survivor movement, and certainly the churches and other spiritual communities can serve either to freeze us in our fear and keep us stuck in our victimization or they can empower us to burst out of the fear-based consciousness that holds us hostage and makes us easy prey for the roaring lion.

So how can we tell if a particular healing resource—a particular therapeutic relationship, twelve-step meeting, survivor's group, or local parish or spiritual community—is freezing us in fear or helping us along in a healing, liberating way? I suggest four questions we can ask ourselves and one another.

1. Is the resource isolating us or connecting us more deeply? We should be suspicious of any program, therapy, church, or movement that draws us away from interest in others, especially those who're different from us.

2. Is the healing resource making us believe we're responsible only for ourselves or is it empowering us to want to learn how to love one another responsibly, in mutually empowering ways? If we've come to believe we can't affect others or change the world and might as well not try, something is wrong. An authentic healing process does not diminish our senses of moral agency or our capacities to believe that we can make a difference.

3. Is the resource making us rigid or is it opening us to per-

sonal change? Something is amiss if we become less able to live with ambiguity, open minds, people who don't always agree with us, or ideas that don't necessarily correspond with our own.

4. Is the healing resource making us self-righteous or is it humbling us and seasoning our compassion, making us more aware of our own capacities to harm others? Even if we are, or have been, victims, we remain hostage to fear if we see ourselves only as victims, powerless and objectified, rather than as subjects of our lives. Regardless of our sex, color, class, sexuality, religion, or whatever abuses we have suffered, we are out of touch with reality unless we are in touch with our own capacities to do harm. Stuck in a sense of victimization, we carry and spread despair and, in so doing, embody the depth of faithlessness that is shattered, in the christian story, by Pentecost.

As the old story unfolds, we're told the people were "cut to the heart." They asked what they could do and were told by Peter and the other disciples to repent, be baptized, and receive the Holy Spirit. We are told that "fear came upon every soul; and that many wonders and signs were done. . . . " We're told that "all who believed were together and held all things in common" and that "they sold their possessions and goods and distributed them to all, as any had need." We're told that "day by day they attended the temple together and broke bread in the homes," that they "partook of food with glad and generous hearts, and praised God," and that "God added to their numbers day by day" (Acts 2:37, 38, 43–47).

This says to me that the gift of sacred Spirit (be it to christians who celebrate Pentecost or among all who are open to the Spirit) is a gift that transforms our lives. And everything changes. We dream dreams. We see visions. Whether we are touched by the Spirit through the church, through therapy or twelve-step programs, through survivor movements, or through other healing or liberation resources, we see that the sacred connects us in mutually empowering ways.

We see that She empowers us to live together creatively and compassionately as sisters and brothers, as friends and companions, as lovers and partners.

We see that She opens us, inviting us to be open with one another to processes of radical personal and social transformation. Our values and commitments, our relationships and work, are re-created as we learn to see that as a people, as earth creatures, and as a body of friends, we do indeed "hold all things in common."

We need to be building our lives in this society on the basis of such a vision. We need to be learning how to live with one another and how to share in one another's well-being or ill-being. We need to be learning how our resources could be organized and distributed. In these days, this is a utopian vision, an image of a socialized economy and health-care system; of nonabusive business and professional practices; of a genuinely just and humane world. We should be learning and teaching, more and more, about how, concretely, to help move our society in this direction, even as the dominant principalities and powers are pulling fiercely in opposition.

And in smaller ways as well, we can learn together what it means to affirm the "I live in you, and you in me," and that because our lives are connected at the root, we will try to do what is right *with* one another. We will try to help keep one another safe. We will try to tend to one another's well-being. And the gift of the Spirit, far from making it clear to me that I am righteous or nonabusive, will help me confess my capacity to do harm, to pose danger to you as well as to myself, and to see, therefore, my need, with you and others, to struggle toward shaping ethical foundations that will help us live together with respect, justice, and compassion.

People who are seriously interested in ethics—in doing the right thing—know that we do, and will, make mistakes and that we need to learn from them. An ethic of risk, of radical

love, is not therefore an ethic that promotes a desire for perfection or a need for certainty, it is an ethic that leads us into
repentance, compassion, and forgiveness. It is an ethic that
opens us to personal and social change.

In October of 1990, my mother phoned from North Carolina to say that her good friend Gini had just told her that Oliver, her oldest child, a graphic artist in his mid-thirties living
in New York City, had AIDS. Gini said to Mama that, when
she got back from visiting Oliver in New York, she wanted
to get with her to talk. Before this conversation could take
place, however, Oliver died. Over Thanksgiving vacation
that fall, my family and I went to visit Gini.

While we were with her, Gini told us about Oliver's life in
New York, his lover and friends, his work and his death. She
spoke of her immense sadness in losing this beloved son and
also of the depth of the caring that had taken place among her
four other children, Oliver's friends, and herself during the
last days of his life. She mentioned having walked across
Manhattan to mail her absentee vote for Harvey Gantt in his
race for the United States Senate against Jesse Helms.

After a while, she said to my mother, "Mary Ann, I want
to say something to you in front of your children. When we
heard about Carter's lesbianism about ten years ago, Bill and
I said to each other that we ought to tell you and Bob about
Oliver. We figured it would help you feel less alone as parents of a gay child. But we couldn't bring ourselves to talk
about it. I want to ask your forgiveness today."

My mother responded immediately, "Gini, that's all right.
We get to these things when we're able to." And she paused
and said, "But there's something I want to ask you. How did
you feel when our friends who'd voted for Jesse Helms came
to Oliver's memorial service?"

Gini replied, "Well, Mary Ann, I'm glad you asked me
that. You know, in the past you've been the one to raise these

issues with our friends, but I want you to know that this is changing. I don't expect our friends to agree with us about everything, but I do expect them, if they are really our friends, to open their minds and struggle with what has been happening in our families."

"I wonder why so many of them have such closed minds," my mother queried. "Mary Ann," Gini said, "It's because they haven't been blessed the way we have been, that's why."

And my mother and Gini proceeded to talk a little more about this blessing. It was not that lesbian and gay children are a greater blessing than other children, it was that these two white, southern, christian, middle-class ladies, one a Presbyterian, one an Episcopalian, have discovered that the sacred Spirit really does touch our lives in special ways in relation to those who are most despised or trivialized, feared or outcast, in our midst.

What happened for Gini, for my mother, for many of us in this place, and for many others, is that in the spirit of Pentecost the old order is being blown apart. Traditional boundaries are giving way. Languages with which we once were at home are being rendered unintelligible. This is not a safe place to be. But it is a place near the heart of God.

6

Finding Our Voices
At the Ordination of a Gay Brother

"When they deliver you up, do not be anxious how you are to speak or what you are to say; for what you are to say will be given to you in that hour; for it is not you who speak, but the Spirit of God speaking through you" (Matt. 10:19–20).

There is a bishop, many years retired, who helped me learn to speak. This bishop, known in various quarters of the church simply as DeWitt, lives today with his spouse on an island off the coast of Maine about six miles, as the crow flies, from Bev's and my little place on Deer Isle. For the last few years, Bishop DeWitt and I have met to talk at breakfast most summers in a local dining spot. Sitting with this lovely, justice-seeking, good-humored man is a spiritual high for me because it helps secure my grounding in this world, its people and other creatures, and the sacred character of our physical, sensual, daily lives in relation to one another.

Bishop DeWitt and three other bishops were censured by the House of Bishops for ordaining women to the priesthood in 1974 before the church had authorized it. With this man, I am reminded that whatever is most genuinely human—most fully just—reveals whatever is most fully divine among us. And this sacred power is sacred *because* it is shared.

Bob DeWitt has been a spiritual mentor to me, not primarily because he is a bishop or even because he ordained my sisters and me at a time when others would not, but rather because all along he has stood with us as his sisters. DeWitt saw, and called forth in us, that spiritual power which we are born to share, generate, celebrate, and pass on. With us, he believed this to be at the heart of christian vocation, the essence of lay and ordained ministry. When someone sees and calls forth this sacred power in us, we often respond by growing more fully into our spiritual stature as sisters and brothers who are on this earth by the power of the Spirit to participate in creating, liberating, and blessing the world.

This, I believe, is what the priesthood is all about: this seeing and calling forth—this speaking, in which it is not simply we who speak but the Spirit speaking through us that calls us, paradoxically, more fully into ourselves.

And yet, the fact is, Barry, this priesthood into which you are being ordained today is a theologically and ethically dubious order that you, I, Jack Spong, Bob DeWitt, and others share. The priesthood is an order cluttered with spiritual, moral, economic, sexual, and other abuses that are intrinsic to the exercise of an unchanging power over others in the name of a deity that is not God at all but a projection of men's control needs. That you are a gay man, Barry, open and unashamed, delighted and radiant in your vocation and that I am a lesbian in no way removes us from the spiritual, moral, and political clutter of the ordained priesthood as a hierarchical order of ministry. Our openly gay and lesbian identity as priests *does* signal that we have a special opportunity to help move the church from its hierarchical power basis toward a more truly sacramental, pastoral, and prophetic community of sisters, brothers, and friends.

We are theological deviants and spiritual resisters less because we are gay and lesbian than because we are *out*. We celebrate, make visible, bear public witness to the connection between power relationships and abuse, between fear and ha-

tred, between our sexual lives and our spiritual commitments, between our passion for sexual and gender justice and
our insistence that racism (including our own), class elitism
(including our own), and the many other structures of injustice in which we wallow, usually unaware, be resisted and
transformed with the same spirit that moves us to declare
that heterosexism, homophobia, sexism, and misogyny have
no place at the christian table. This holy Spirit compels us to
declare that, as priests of the church, we will not tolerate
these sins against gay men, lesbians, and (if the truth be
known) all women, especially those who dare to share,
claim, and celebrate our creative, liberating power as the
power of God.

If we make these connections and commit ourselves to
such a God, we will be transforming the church at its roots,
just as we ourselves will be transformed by the One who is
calling us and speaking through us.

For some time, we christians have been in the midst of another Reformation which many are beginning to realize.[1]
And this Reformation is not only about whether the churches
will ordain sexually active homosexuals and bless our relationships, it is also about whether women and men priests,
bishops, laypersons, and deacons will continue to acquiesce
to the patriarchal structures, language, and theologies of the
church and whether we as women will continue on as "female patriarchs"—mothers and daughters of a father who
alone knows what's best for his world.

We are in a Reformation with roots in a shared realization
that patriarchal religion with its origins in unchanging power
relationships will not do, even when the power is being exer-
cised benevolently and with good intention, as is the case
with church leaders, ordained and lay, who mean well and
want to do what's right—people like most of us.[2] Structures
of power in which certain people—usually (not always)

white, straight (or closeted) affluent males—shape the destinies and control the lives of others will not do, even when they are set in place to serve the common good. This presumably was the effort of leaders in the former Soviet Union. Perhaps it is the case also in our own White House and in the military, economic, and technological structures of our lives that leave us increasingly numb with powerlessness and fatigue.

Lay and ordained ministers in this period of Reformation should embody, with every breath, a compassionate challenge to this sense of powerlessness that hangs over us like a pall. The danger we are facing finally may be less that of nuclear war than that we women and men, we children and old people, we lighter and darker earth creatures, we whales and eagles and sparrows, we willows and roses and chickweed will have no more air, no more food, no more voice, no more capacity to keep on keepin' on, to smile, or even to weep.

Hear the poetic voice of our brother Louie Crew, a gorgeous queen among us: "The tree, the sky and the water were ours / we presumed, for us to use as we pleased / as if we had a Visacard or Mastercharge account / in God's name with no payment to make in our generation."[3]

Jesus asked what it profits any of us to gain the world at the expense of our souls—our right-connectedness to other creatures as our brothers and sisters. We priests need to hold up before our sisters and brothers the serious moral question of what has happened to the *soul* of this nation—our sacred connection with, and shared responsibility for, one another's well-being—especially those most cruelly and contemptuously cast aside as expendable to the dominant social order: poor people, homeless people, many people of color, lesbian and gay men, sick people, people with AIDS, the elderly, women and children of all colors, especially poor women and children of color, and of course, other earth and sea and air creatures. We Reformation priests, ordained and lay, need to be helping shape the soul of a nation that has lost it and that, in fact, has never had a soul as deep and broad, as expansive and courageous, as inclusive and compassionate, as the one we so badly need today.

The Reformation is occurring today because folks who haven't been nourished physically, emotionally, mentally, or spiritually are breaking the silence and speaking words that are hard to hear because they call us all, every one of us, not just our enemies, to a spiritual "turning," conversion, the work of personal and social transformation. Our own lives, not just those of others, must be toppled.

We christian priests are being called to speak such words carefully and caringly, to be "wise as serpents, and innocent as doves," we are told, in such a way that we are giving God her voices in this world.

Barry asked me to preach because he wanted a gay or lesbian voice to be heard today and he asked me to say something about how we find our voices. And so I want to name and comment briefly on what I see to be four signs of sacred voices, that is, of how we may know it is God speaking through us and others rather than self-delusions or pseudo-sacred spirits passing themselves off for divine.

First, the voices of God always call us more fully into *mutually empowering relationship* in which all parties are taken seriously and enabled more fully to be true selves. This is what justice making is. God calls us into this dynamic relational way of being with one another in which our relationships, whether as groups or individuals, are never fixed permanently but rather are open to ongoing transformation. The revolution truly is never won.

A common distortion of God's voices, as historically they have been transmitted by the church, is that it is one voice spoken "from above." It is spoken "down" to us: the voice of the Pope, the Bishop, the Priest, the Preacher, the President, the one in charge. Even when spoken as a benevolent voice, this hierarchal power, insofar as it represents an unchanging, static relationship between God and his/her people or between the priest and his/her people is not a sacred voice at all but rather that of an idol created to hold patriarchal power in place. And this is what makes the ordained priesthood such a spiritually precarious vocation. For, like the church, it is a patriarchal institution. We cannot deny this or pretend it is not so and be honest people. I call you, Barry, to participate in reforming the priesthood and the church.

Second, God speaks *embodied, sensual words,* their sources rich in human history and deep in the earth, our planet home. These are voices of honesty and passion, voices genuinely seeking mutuality, heartily speaking for justice. These sacred voices get erased in the church through the promulgation of a false spirituality that derives its basis from the longstanding anti-female and anti-sexual agenda of all patriarchal religion, christianity being no exception. It is no wonder that sexuality is such a major issue for the churches these days! Insofar as these matters of sex, gender, and power are being resolved on the side of an embodied, sensual justice for us all, the theological foundations of the church will be shifting. We are discovering what it means that the Holy One is no more a father than a sister, no more a mother than a brother, no more a creator and a redeemer than a passionate lover and a beloved friend. And this is very good. We are meeting, in ways new to many of us, the God whom Jesus loved; the One whose relational dynamic shone—and shines—through not only the brother from Nazareth but through all who seek justice, love, mercy, and walk humbly in the Spirit.

The bogus hype about the size of the gay male hypothalamus notwithstanding, gay/lesbian life, politics, and spirituality does not originate solely for many (if any) of us in either biology or destiny but rather in our willingness in this historical moment to respond to a sacred call, insofar as we can, together. The theory that gay men or lesbians are "born homosexual" is, I believe, a way of keeping the issue of homosexuality containable and far away from those who want badly to believe that they were born *heterosexual*. In fact, our sexual morality, whether we are gay, straight, or bisexual, whether we are sexually active or celibate, has as much to do with where we put our lives as where we put our genitals. Our sexual morality is about how deeply, honestly, and creatively we are connected with the world and how we express this. Our morality as sexual creatures is about how committed we are to seeking and finding nonviolent, nonabusive ways of relating to one another.

The church's expectation that we will lie about our lives, through words or silence, is an *ethic of flagrant duplicity, and this ethic is sexually immoral.* For individual gay men and lesbians to go along with this duplicity is frequently a means of survival, or perhaps to buy time to break free later when, we hope, we can move from a position of greater strength and clarity. But our closeted sisters and brothers need to be aware that the closet is a container designed to impede the movement of an erotically empowering sacred Spirit and to silence her voices.

And so the big moral question for lesbians and gay men seeking ordination or those already ordained (and our numbers are legion) is not whether we should abstain from sexual activity but whether we will continue to be silenced by the church's duplicity.

A friend of mine, Mariel Kinsey, a psychotherapist in the Boston area, has written a poem in which she says, "it's what we turn our backs on/that finally comes and stares us down."[4]

For many generations, the church has turned its back on erotically empowered and empowering women and on the earthiness and sensuality of who we women, men, and other earth creatures are together. Today, especially through the lives of lesbian, gay, and bisexual christians, this sacred power has come to face us. I call you, Barry, as my brother and as an openly gay and sexually active priest to join in staring us down.

Third, the voices of God are not solo voices. God sings with and through us all. The primary reason that twelve-step programs have become so important to so many of us is that the healing power sparked and generated in the meetings of groups like AA, NA, and OA is a radically shared power, not really "higher" at all.

A serious problem in modern protestantism is that we have bought theologically into the social and economic basis of capitalism—a radical individualism—as the alpha and omega of what it means to be human. This terribly false, morally bankrupt, spiritual cooptation needs desperately to be challenged in and by the churches, and it has not been, in any major way, by the protestant churches in the United States or elsewhere.

In this period following the collapse of totalitarian-style communism in Europe and the Soviet Union, we western christians need to be alert to the possibility that our primary mission, as church, may be to become a common body, ourselves sisters and brothers, we and other creatures with us.

I call you, Barry, to do all you can to help shape a vision of our common good and to do what you can to teach, preach, and celebrate creative resistance to the dominant theology of advanced monopoly capitalism that has taught us falsely that we are on our own and that such matters as how we make or spend money, what gods we worship, who we sleep with, and what we value are simply our own private business.

Fourth, because the voices of God are seasoned in our commonness, our connectedness as a body of brothers and sisters, they are voices of *compassion*. We are here on the earth to learn with one another how, genuinely, to love our enemies as well as our friends in ways that do not disregard or deny our anger at oppression, our passion for justice, and our impatience with duplicity and lies. Like love, compassion is not a sentiment. It is a radical act of seeing our relatedness as creatures and of attempting to embody this relation in mutually empowering ways.

Make no mistake. Compassionate voices do not suffer fools gladly or pay lip-service to a god of love and peace at the expense of the sacred struggle for justice. But this kind of morally soft, tasteless, spiritual pablum is exactly what most of us white middle-strata christians have learned to associate with love and compassion. It is a spirituality we must unlearn together. I call you, Barry, to help us unlearn this false spirituality. Be open yourself to the Spirit that grounds us in compassion. Embrace the One who seasons us in humility, opening us to receiving forgiveness for the wrongs that we do and to forgiving those who genuinely are repentant.

Strange as it may seem, there really are lots of brothers and sisters in the church who truly believe that the God of all creation, the Spirit of life that moves through the cosmos, actually cares whether we are gay, lesbian, straight, or bisexual; male or female; christian, Muslim, Jew, Buddhist, or wicca. There really are folks who believe God "prefers" heterosexual to homosexual sex and who will go to great lengths to impose "God's preference," which is really their own, upon everyone. I believe the hardest part of compassion, that which reflects the passion and suffering of God, is to be open to forgiving those who cannot receive this forgiveness because they are not repentant. They do not see or believe that they have done anything wrong, anything to hurt, wound, or violate us or others.

This is where we gay and lesbian christians find ourselves today insofar as the Spirit is working through us. We do not deny our ongoing need for repentance and forgiveness for such sins as our own greed, our duplicity, our racism, and the harm that we do others through our internalized homophobia and misogyny. At the same time, we are ready to forgive those brothers and sisters, in this church and elsewhere, who exclude and patronize, wound and violate, us and others and who do not know what they are doing. They do not know that through their fear, confusion, and often their barely veiled hatred, they are breaking the Body of Christ, which is our body and their own body.

Is this not what Jesus meant when he asked God to forgive his brothers and sisters—"for they do not know what they do"? This yearning to forgive is, I believe, at the very heart of God, and it is the basis of sacred reformation.

So here we stand—we can do no other. May we not forget that it is no one of us standing here alone or, except momentarily, out in front of the others. Various ones will be called forth from time to time to lead as best we can: Louie Crew, Kim Byham, Betsy Hess, Ellen Barrett, Robert Williams, David Norgard, Anne Gilson, Elizabeth Carl, Claudia Windal, to name a few, come to mind, and those in solidarity with us, too, folks like Jack Spong, Paul Moore, George Hunt, Jack and Marilyn Croneberger, Barbara Harris, Sue Hiatt, and Mary Lou Suhor.[5]

Individuals will come and go. But the victory is being won because we are standing *together,* giving voices to a God who was with us in the beginning and will be with us in the end, staring us down and holding us up.

7

Healing Together
Homily at an AIDS Healing Service

Last night, I decided with my vet to end the life of my splendid cat-without-a-tail, Sam.[1] Later, today, I'll go to be with Sam, to hold him as life slips away and to let him go into death. Losing anyone, human or any creature we have loved, is sad. And there is no good way to erase the sadness, not if we are fully and deeply human; no way not to feel sadness and grief in the presence of death; no way not to feel sadness or fear in the presence of any life-threatening situation or illness, such as AIDS.

My cat Sam cannot be "cured." Yet I hope and believe that there can be some healing today, some authentic empowerment, some spiritual comforting—strengthening—for Sam and for me in a shared experience of how genuinely we have cared for each other and, now, are letting go.

With Sam on my mind I've come here, imagining that many of you also come with particular relationships on your minds—relationships in which healing is needed: healing of person, healing of relationships, healing of so much of creation groaning under the weight of disease, tragedy, and violence in the larger and smaller places of our life together on earth.

A healing theme connects this morning's readings from

Romans and John. The theme runs through all sacred material in our lives. It is the theme of our being related to one another—sisters, brothers, friends—in and by the power of the One who creates, redeems, and sustains us. Which is to say, we are not alone, nor are we really on our own, responsible primarily for ourselves, accountable primarily to ourselves. We are created, and creative, in connection with one another, those present and absent, those past, present, and future, human creatures, other creatures. And therein—in this connectedness, in our relatedness—is the sacred root of our power to heal and be healed. This is the root of all christian vocation, the root of the church, this power of God-with-us-and-through-us to touch, to heal, to raise the dead.

And Paul asks the Romans: "If God is for us, who can be against us?" He raises this question in the context of what have become notorious theological assumptions about "predestination" and "election," but what he was trying to do at the time he was writing was to locate the place of christian witness in a violent, secular society not unlike our own.

So, how *are* we christians to understand *our* place in this world, as healers and liberators, without falling into arrogant and deadly lies about our exclusivity in the eyes of God?

The doctrine of election too often has been interpreted as a doctrine of exclusivity and superiority, a teaching that signals the church's set-apartness and set-aboveness in relation to the world. In fact, nothing could be less true. No theological statement, including biblical claims, can be understood truthfully and creatively outside the historical, social contexts in which they were made. Paul's discussion of election and of christian set-apartness cannot be understood outside the context of oppression and persecution of the christians to whom he was writing. Paul was speaking of and to a situation in which folks were suffering because they had chosen—elected —to stand with one another against Roman persecution.

Chosen to stand together in suffering. Elected to be healers, liberators.

It is an altogether different matter—spiritually, morally, and politically—for oppressed and persecuted people to believe that God is suffering with them than for U.S. citizens to believe that God won with us in the Persian Gulf war. To experience God suffering with us can season our faith in the Spirit of vulnerability and compassion. To imagine that God reigns victorious over people and creatures that have experienced massive suffering and death is to foster a theology of conquest, control, and violence. It is to pay homage to a most unholy spirit.

At root, the doctrine of election is about *human* choice. For all are called, but not all choose to stand with one another, in vulnerability and compassion, accompanying one another through pain, fear, loss, and suffering, sharing power that is sacred because it is shared. All are called, but not all choose to heal and be healed. For we cannot be healers unless we are being touched and healed in the Spirit through which we participate in bringing others to new life.

And if we are healers, nothing can separate us from the love of God because, healed and healing, calling one another to life, together we are embodying that which is fully divine—and with and through us, fully human or creaturely: God all rolled up in us and we, in God. In this co-inherence, we become more fully ourselves.

Through this lens of co-inherence—God in us, we in God—the Fourth Gospel suggests the meaning of Jesus' life, death, and ongoing—resurrected—presence with us: He is redemptively—christically—bound up with us: He in us, we in him. Our lives are connected at the root of the creation we share: divinity and humanity, we and other earth creatures, all of us participants, interdependent and mutual, in our living and dying. To realize and celebrate our radical connectedness as brothers, sisters, and friends is to share the bread of life—christic power, sacred spirit, power of God—by which we are fed and by which we heal together.

So we come here today, a sick and broken body, ravished by the AIDS virus and varieties of physical, mental, and other personal ailments and battered by social, economic, and political forces among us: racism, heterosexism, sexism, capitalism, militarism, religious and cultural imperialism, able-bodyism and ageism, and certainly a "species-ism" that puts humankind alone at the center of God's interest and our own. Greed and fear have become our national and ecclesiastic idols, and we all are hungry for healing in this historical moment of spiritual and ethical famine.

We come seeking healing—spiritual food for ourselves and others, our nation and others, the world and the church. Insofar as we are actively in solidarity with those who are suffering and have compassion with and for one another, including our enemies, we not only *share* the bread of life, we *become* the bread of life, by the power of the Spirit who, in joining us with one another, empowers us to share in feeding, healing, and liberating the world.

8

At a Vigil for a Gay Man Badly Beaten

On Wednesday morning, one of my students, a lesbian and a friend, told me that a man—the police thought it was David G., a gay brother and former student—had been savagely bashed in the head with a hammer. For a moment I was stunned, trying to take in this dreadful news. I was saddened. I was outraged. But I was *not* in the least surprised.

I am not surprised when gay men and lesbians are assaulted just as I am not surprised when people of color, Jews, other racial, ethnic, or religious minorities are attacked, when women are raped and battered, when children are abused, when animals are treated with unspeakable cruelty. These vicious, violent times are steeped in a fear that seeks scapegoats and destroys them. Violence against queers like David and so many of us is no accident. It is a predictable and purposeful part of a sexual, racial, and economic order built upon the violated bodies and spirits of all who are, in any way, "deviant" from the white, ostensibly heterosexual, male who aspires to be economically and otherwise in control of his life, his family, and his world.

We need to be clear that the person or persons who smashed in David's head were not isolated individuals out of touch with the prevailing values and customs of our society.

The assailant was not out of touch with reality. He (and I am sure, in this case, it was a "he") was embodying the dominant values and customs of our society and its major institutions such as the christian church and the U.S. military. The attacker was not a social aberration, a mistake, but rather a representative of the attitudes being held up as "all-American" and as "good christian" and "family" values.

It's all connected—the spiritual and psychological and physical damage, the economic and sexual and racial exploitation. I suspect that the Fenway bashers, like most people who beat up queers, believe that they're acting on behalf of God and country. And why shouldn't they? Have you read the Roman Catholic church's recent declaration that homosexuality is "intrinsically evil"? If something is evil, why not bash it?

There is a direct psychological and social link between the homophobic rantings of the Joint Chiefs of Staff and what happened to David and at least eight other men in this part of Boston since late July. And there is a deep, disturbing connection between the christian churches' despicable teachings on women, sex, and homosexuality and gay bashing, an insidious, wicked relationship between the beatings and burnings and other hate crimes perpetrated against us and the negation of our sexual being—the passion in our souls and bodies—by the christian church and other patriarchal religions, too.

Any creed that permits, much less justifies, discrimination does in fact foster violence. And that's where we are today, in the midst of a violent culture being cultivated by church and state. This is an evil situation and we need to name it so, speaking publicly about the religious and political roots of queer bashing; speaking boldly with an anger and a compassion that threatens to transform the world by the sheer force of our commitment to justice making with compassion in a world in which justice and compassion seem largely to have vanished from most peoples' dreams of what is possible.

More than anything, my friends, you and I are called by the spirit of life, the force for love making, the power that moves the struggles for justice and compassion in history; we are called to believe that it is possible to change the world by the force of a love that is stronger than fear. And our belief in this possibility, this force, this love *is* our strength.

When we consider what has happened to our brothers recently, to David and the others, we need to be mindful that their assailants are tormented people acting out fear and hatred they have learned in a tormented society. These perpetrators of violence, like the society they mirror, need to be judged. *The violence must be stopped, and violent people must be held accountable for the evil they do.* But, like all of us, they need to be healed—their fears transformed to courage and their power to do evil transformed to a force for contrition, repentance, sorrow, and love.

And so, those who pray need to do so not only for David G. and other victims of violence but also for the assailants, and for ourselves. We need to pray that all of us—in this park, at the altars of our churches, in the sanctuaries of other places of worship, in the State House, the White House, the Congress, and the Pentagon—all of us may be touched and transformed by the spirit of compassion and courage, which is our only hope.

Remembering My Father
Gentle, Whimsical Man, Lousy Patriarch

I'm delighted to be here this morning with this remarkable organization, Parents and Friends of Lesbians and Gays. I'm also pleased to be here with Harvey Gantt[1] who, for so many, has become a symbol of integrity and courage and hope. As in the story of David and Goliath, I see Jesse Helms and the massive corporate, economic, political, and military structure he represents as the supergiant Goliath posing as a friend to the little people, hardworking men and women. And I see what Harvey Gantt embodies—his commitments to justice and his compassion—as the little David of a story that isn't over.

For we[2] here in fact are shaping the story with our lives, and it is not simply a tale about the struggle for sexual equality, for the rights of gay men and lesbians. We are struggling also for women of all colors; for African American, Native American, Hispanic, and Asian American men, women, and children. We are interested not simply in sharing the power, privileges, and prestige of affluent white, ostensibly heterosexual males in this society, ours is a struggle for justice and compassion—for transformation of the society into a time and place in which violence, abuse, and poverty are no more; a social order in which racism, sexism, heterosexism, anti-

Semitism, and the savaging of the earth are no longer economic requirements as they are today.

I hope that what I am sharing this morning will spark images of how we, unlike David, might tame the mighty giant rather than kill him. Killing enemies is, after all, a very patriarchal way of handling conflict—patriarchy being the historical pattern of ordering society on the basis of men's relationships of domination, control, and the exercise of an unchanging power over others—other men, women, children, animals, and the earth. A nonpatriarchal, or feminist, re-imaging of the drama of David and Goliath might present it as a story of taming—of befriending and disarming—the giant.

In this spirit, you and I are called to participate in taming giants, in healing and liberating the world around us and within us—a world teeming with tragedy and disease such as AIDS and with evil such as racism, sexism, capitalist greed and violence, able-bodyism, anti-Semitism, anti-Arabism, and heterosexism.

As a way of imaging how we might work together as healers and liberators, I want to focus on my relationship with my father. I want to share in this way at this particular gathering because I believe it is an appropriate occasion for a child to honor a parent who honored her and to invite the rest of you, if you will, to "read" yourselves between these lines.

During the latter years of his life and since his death in 1984, I've come to experience the relationship—between myself, a lesbian daughter, and my father, Bob Heyward, a moderately conservative, straight, christian man—as a source of psychospiritual empowerment. We didn't have the sort of father-daughter relationship Hollywood or Wall Street would have been especially interested in. My father was not an "all-American" head of family, super-achiever, go-getter, and I was not a dutiful daughter who did what she was told.[3]

Like other real relationships, ours was more complicated, at times cluttered with pain and confusion. Still, for both of us, it was a significant resource of healing and liberation, a parent-child connection that became increasingly over time a mutually empowering relationship, which is as fully as we will come in this life to experiencing the power of God.

I've come home to Charlotte to do some remembering. Before turning to my father, I want to say a word about my mother, Mary Ann Carter Heyward. Like most of you, my mother grew up in a society in which sexuality was a taboo issue, as it continues to be among many folks. It is certainly not that my mother never experienced in herself the fear and confusion about sexuality that so often results in closed minds and tightly set religious principles. She has known the fear and confusion and at times still does. But she is a woman with a generosity of spirit and an openness to change and difference, and her faith calls her to risk looking beyond the conventional, with which she often feels most at home herself. My mother and I are still in process, growing and changing together, as mother and daughter, and as friends and companions, as we do our best to make some small differences in the world around us.

My father was a lousy patriarch. Because patriarchy is a system of domination and control, a "good" patriarch is a man (or a woman seeking patriarchal power) for whom power means control, possession, entitlement, power over others. Patriarchal power is epitomized by violence—explicit violence such as war, rape, child abuse, battering of partners, and the ravishing of natural resources through indifference, ignorance, and greed. More implicitly, patriarchal power is epitomized by the use of professional position or of status, age, race, gender, class, sexual identity, or other power differentials as a means of intimidating, embarrassing, diminishing, extorting favors, or otherwise exercising control.[4]

A lousy patriarch is a someone who doesn't buy fully into this experience of this power hierarchy. My father was such a guy. Breaking rank with patriarchy, he attempted to pass on to his children several blessings that reflect a different experience of power—an experience of our creative power as shared and mutual, represented brilliantly in the AIDS quilt, an image of our connectedness in life and death. I want to reflect on this transformative power and to name some of its blessings: an openness to change; spiritual depth and simplicity; a sense of humor; and an awareness that loving involves setting free.

OPENNESS TO CHANGE

Patriarchs know it all. It is in the character of a good patriarch not to change his mind—not to be a "wimp"—because, after all, since he is right, he has nothing to learn, no reason to change. As Margaret Mead reportedly reflected on the attitude of a man who'd gone to observe the native inhabitants of a remote island: "His mind was made up, and he did not wish to have it changed by interactions with the people." Such an attitude is quintessentially patriarchal.

In 1974, before the church had authorized the ordination of women, eleven of us Episcopal women deacons were ordained to the priesthood. This event left the Episcopal church reeling. It also signaled a crisis throughout the churches, protestant and catholic, that had been under way for some time: a crisis about how the churches understand, and what the churches will do about, the faith claims of women and of openly gay, lesbian, and bisexual sisters and brothers. For the next several generations (we are in the midst of it now), the churches would become a battleground between those bearing witness to how the God whom Jesus loved may be inviting us to experience sacred, erotically empowering, justice-seeking, compassionate love and those who are clear that God's commandments are being flagrantly violated by such groups as P-FLAG and certainly by gay and lesbian christians.

From the outset of the movement for women's ordination,

my father was an advocate of women priests and was puzzled by the church's resistance. Through this struggle in the church, so much a part of my life for a number of years, I came to recognize in Daddy a mind that was remarkably open and free of patriarchal assumptions about the relationship between God and gender. I began to see that he had always been open, if often slow to change, open even in situations in which he'd have been more comfortable staying closed.

For example, the preacher at this controversial ordination was Dr. Charles Willie, a professor at the Harvard School of Education and an eloquent African American lay leader in the Episcopal Church. Dr. Willie preached a powerful sermon on this occasion in which he compared women's refusal in 1974 to be complicit in our oppression with Rosa Parks's refusal in 1954 to go to the back of the bus in Montgomery. A month or two after the service, Dr. Willie and I ran into each other in Cambridge and he said to me something like this: "Carter, your father is a most remarkable man! He came up to me after the ordination in Philadelphia and said, 'Dr. Willie. Bob Heyward here, Carter's father, and I want to say something to you: I was born and raised in South Carolina and taught certain things about black people and white people. I always truly believed it would be wrong for me to entertain a black person in my home or allow my children to bring their black friends to my home. And, when I heard you speak today, I realized how wrong I've been all my life about these things. I want you to know, Dr. Willie, that I'd be proud to have you in my home.'"

Charles Willie said he was startled and deeply touched by my father's confession. I, too, was surprised (Daddy hadn't mentioned this to me) and moved. My father's passing on to his kids this legacy of an openness to change was a blessing from which, I pray, I will draw forever.

SPIRITUAL DEPTH AND SIMPLICITY

It is important to recognize that change did not come easily for my father, as often it does not for people with open minds. Daddy was not tossed and blown across the surface of life, battered back and forth by the winds of opinion. My father's psychospiritual moorings were simple and deep. The story of his conversion by Dr. Willie is not about spontaneous change but rather about the culmination of a long spiritual struggle about race and racism. Similarly, in relation to my lesbian sexuality, my father's affirmation did not come easily for him or me. It evolved over time. By the time of his death, he had pretty much made peace with my life and was pleased with my primary relational commitment to Bev, a woman he much admired.

In June, 1979, I came out as a lesbian by publishing a couple of articles in progressive christian journals.[5] As it happened, I was scheduled to speak in November at Myers Park Baptist Church in Charlotte at the invitation of the Women of the Church,[6] an invitation sustained by the pastor Gene Owens and most lay leaders of the church after my sexuality became a matter of public record. In this context, the *Charlotte Observer*'s Frye Gaillard interviewed me and my parents, who shone like beacons in their refutation of Anita Bryant's bigotry as "unchristian."[7] Reading from a prepared text for both Mama and himself, Daddy said something like this: "While her mother and I certainly do not understand or approve of Carter's lifestyle, we know that she is a responsible person who does not take such matters lightly. We love her and respect her and pray for the wisdom to understand."

My parents saw that what matters is not whether they (or we) "understand" or "approve" of all things but that we respect and love one another and, therefore, that we are open to, and praying for, the wisdom to understand whatever may confuse or trouble us.

This way of being runs contrary to patriarchal expectations. Patriarchs do not go deeply into spiritual matters. They cannot or they would begin to tap into the divine/human roots of their own pain and of a yearning for mutuality and connectedness. In order to avoid this reckoning, which would spark new values, new commitments, and new life, patriarchs must stay on the surface and therefore be preoccupied with appearance. (Make a mental note that this is a primary source of our notions of cosmetic beauty as well as, for girls and women in this society, of such diseases as anorexia nervosa and bulimia.) Without much spiritual depth, patriarchs lack the roots that would give them much personal security, peace of mind, and integrity/wholeness as persons.

By contrast, my father had spiritual depth. He was not preoccupied with others' opinions of him or us. He was not terribly concerned about appearance. I have wondered where Daddy got this spiritual mooring.

He was raised by devout Presbyterian parents and was the youngest of six kids in the economically depressed South. His parents were caring, industrious christian people. His father was a retired military officer whom people still called "The Major" long after World War I had come and gone. He was so strict a disciplinarian, whipping his sons with such regularity, that my father was, in my judgment, a physically abused child. I suspect his psychospiritual roots were in his capacity to dream and hope beyond the economic stress and physical abuse of his own boyhood and the larger society on the basis of some strong sense of connectedness he experienced, but with whom—his siblings? friends? pets? his hard-working father? the stepmother who cared for him? the mother who died when he was six? some teacher? some black man or woman who worked alongside him in the cotton fields? and, later, with my mother and his children?

Somehow my father experienced God as the source of a sense of connectedness that he knew to be sacred—godly—

through acts of relational kindness, openness, and compassion. God was not to him a strict disciplinarian, a major, or a judge, at least not in a primary or necessary way.[8] All of us in this dominant culture surely carry some feeling-images and memories of judgment and violence in our psyches and spiritualities, if only because we inhabit a violent, harshly judging, social order. So, too, my father. But still he managed to embrace a largely nonjudgmental, inclusive christian spirituality.

Who knows exactly how anyone gets cultivated in the soil of human kindness in the midst of a broken world? Who knows, especially, how a man in patriarchy gets rooted more or less securely in an ability to yearn for a better world—and to recognize and celebrate this yearning in his daughters and son? My father left us a legacy of spiritual depth, of simplicity and yearning, a blessing worthy of being shared and passed on from generation to generation.

SENSE OF HUMOR/PERSPECTIVE

A sense of humor is, at heart, a sense of perspective that includes an ability to laugh at oneself. Patriarchy does not teach us how to enjoy ourselves or others, how to relax, how to laugh at ourselves and the incongruities that happen at no one's expense. In 1956, when I was 11; my brother Robbie, 5; and my sister Ann, 4, we had a pet duck we named "Peppy." An Easter present, this duck had arrived as a tiny yellow ball of feathers and legs and grew fairly quickly into a hefty white bird that followed us kids everywhere—including into the house and onto the street where it was likely to meet sudden death.

Against stiff opposition, our father finally persuaded us that Peppy would be happier and safer in the lake at Freedom Park. And so, we agreed reluctantly to take Peppy to the lake some Sunday after church and say goodbye to this feathered friend. The day finally came and we set out—Daddy, Mama,

Nana (our maternal grandmother), Robbie, Ann, Peppy, and me. After church we drove to Freedom Park where Daddy, Robbie, Ann, and I carried Peppy, quacking all the way, from the car to the lake where several dozen big white ducks were swimming or sunning.

"See there!" exclaimed Daddy. "Peppy has got himself a fine home! This is exactly where he belongs. He'll be as happy as can be! Why, by the time we've been gone five minutes, Peppy will have forgotten all about us and will be enjoying his new friends!"

Not convinced, but feeling a little better than we'd imagined, we headed back toward the car. Behind us we heard it: "Quack, Quack, Quack." Sure enough, Peppy was following us. Daddy went running back to the duck, picked Peppy up, and headed back to the lake.

"You folks go on now and get back in the car with Mama and Nana," he yelled, "It'll be easier for Peppy if you're out of sight."

A few minutes later, Daddy arrived back at the car, all smiles, and assured us that Peppy would soon be swimming happily with his friends in the lake.

"Is he doing it yet?" one of us asked. "Well, not quite. I think he misses you but, now that we're gone, he'll be fine. I tell you what, we'll drive around for a few minutes and come back—and you'll see what I mean. Peppy will be out there with all the other ducks and you won't even be able to tell which one he is. *I promise.*"

So we drove around for a while, then headed back to Freedom Park. As we approached, we all gasped at once—for there, running up the middle of the fairly heavily trafficked road, quacking his heart out, was Peppy! And we kids began screaming, "Daddy!! You *promised*!! Daddy!!"

My father often told this story to illustrate one of the many incongruities of parenting. For years after the event, we kids told the story and got our father to recall it with us, because we so loved to hear him talk about Peppy (whom he called

"Quacky") running up the road, quacking, making him eat his promise.

Daddy loved to tell jokes. To this day, my siblings and I share an image of our father laughing until he shook, until we thought his sides would split, and our getting tickled with him and laughing until we began to shake, even when we didn't know what was so funny. We did know it was never cruel or crude, though sometimes his jokes were sexist or racist and we would be annoyed with him. He would fuss and fume about our lack of humor and then would usually apologize or, sometimes, simply would not tell the joke again in front of us.

When he died, several friends wrote to me of his marvelous sense of humor and his beautiful smile. These gifts, too, were part of his legacy.

SETTING FREE

It seems my father knew that, when we love, we set each other free. The most basic condition for patriarchy is that men (and women who aspire to be like them) must stay in control—of themselves and everyone else. They don't share power because for them power is possession, entitlement, that which by definition is not, and cannot be, shared. If it were, it would not be power—i.e., control—it would be friendship. It would be love. It would be, in fact, no one's personal possession.

In 1973, immediately following my ordination as an Episcopal deacon (and six years before I came out as a lesbian), my father was at the reception my friends were having for me in my New York apartment. It was a festive celebration with much toasting going on. In the midst of it all, somebody picked up a copy of *Time* or *Newsweek* that was lying on the coffee table and said it was too bad that Secretariat, the racehorse whose picture was on the cover, didn't seem to want to breed (a prediction that turned out false). My father seized the moment.

I want to toast my daughter, Carter, who's a lot like Secretariat, I think. She's not here to be bred. Some of us are. But she's not. She's here to run a race, and today she's rounded another bend. I want her to know how much I love her and how proud I am to be her daddy. I pray that God will give her the freedom to run.

The possibility of loving enough to set free cannot be celebrated or recognized in patriarchal relationships, precisely because the moment we set those we love free or recognize and affirm their freedom we give up our power over them and become instead their brothers, sisters, and friends. My father managed to convey to his children a love that frees because, somewhere, somehow, he had seen that this is what matters most. His experience of this love meant it got passed on to his kids—enabling us, from our earliest years, to live with some degree of personal freedom. It also enabled our father, whatever he actually felt about what we were doing, to be there for us through our own personal crises and difficult life passages, such as my coming out as a lesbian.

My father and I never did agree about capital punishment. But by the end of his life in 1984, he was down on Ronald Reagan and even further down on Jesse Helms. I suspect, had he lived much longer, he'd have seen that the public's favoring of the death penalty is being generated by the same fear, anger, and sense of powerlessness that gives us presidents, senators, policies, and wars that may make us feel a little safer for a while—as they are edging us toward economic catastrophe, social chaos, and spiritual death. This is where we are today.

It is a dangerous context in which we lesbian, gay, and bisexual people, our parents, and our friends are being called to join in re-creating the world by the power of a love that sets us free.

10

Alienation and Pastoral Care

The Social Basis and Ethical Challenge of Psychospiritual Healing

INTRODUCTION

For much of my life and all of my professional life, now spanning more than twenty-five years, I have been interested in the interplay of emotional and mental health, spiritual struggle and theological discourse, and social and political forces that shape the totality of life. If I had performed half as well in math and chemistry as in "Religion 101" in college (not that I was a great scholar in religion), I might have gone on to medical school and into psychiatry or veterinary medicine rather than into a seminary and contact with folks like Anne and John Bennett, Nelle Morton, Beverly Harrison, Bob Brown, Jim Cone, and Dorothee Sölle. Once at Union Seminary, I could not go home again, could not turn back to a time of intellectual or spiritual innocence. And this has been a great blessing—always to be questioning how our spiritualities, our psyches, our god-talk, our self-esteem, our bodyselves, and the world around us are being shaped by larger social forces. I have come to believe that healing is always a political act—a process required and shaped by the larger context of our lives in society and steeped in power relations between those who participate in the work of healing and those who seek healing or, in modern medical parlance, "treatment."

Like other healers, those of us schooled primarily in religion and theology to be pastors, rabbis, priests, ministers, counselors, and care-givers on the whole have learned little about the politics of our work. Clinical Pastoral Education (CPE), for over forty years the professional ground of clinical training for clergy, has made little effort to re-form itself through a recognition of power relations in hospitals, prisons, or parishes—or of the political roles of hospitals, prisons, and parishes in contemporary society. In 1972, when I did a unit of CPE in a girls reform school, there was hardly a mention of racism, classism, or sexism as having anything to do with why the girls were in the reform school or with what we chaplains might need to be aware of in our work as pastoral care givers in an institution filled with poor black and brown adolescent females. That was more than two decades ago. But I understand it hasn't changed all that much. CPE is basically about learning to be "pastoral," not about politics or controversy except in extraordinary circumstances.

My essay examines how we understand and embody the work of healing, especially those of us who are pastoral care givers. By "pastoral care," I mean a psychospiritual process of accompanying other persons through hard times, great and small, a process that we experience and recognize as spiritual, emotional, political, and social. We tend to think of pastoral care primarily as engagement with individuals. It can and should also be a dimension of good classroom teaching, community organizing, administration, social action, and advocacy.

I want to help raise consciousness about important, intrinsic connections between power relations and pastoral care. I want to suggest that pastoral care is a process that should clarify, rather than obfuscate, the source of so much of our pain in structures of alienation such as classism, racism, and hetero/sexism. The first section of my essay, therefore, is on "alienation," which we need to understand as the context within which all healing—of body, psyche, and spirit—occurs. Unless we understand the depth of the problem of alienation, the extent to which it shapes our lives, there is no way we can work effectively as pastors. The second section is on pastoral care as a dimension of the theo-ethical work of resistance to injustice and of social transformation.

ALIENATION

One of the earliest feeling/memories from my childhood was a sadness in the air, a "cloud" that would seem to come from out of nowhere and hover over my family and me from time to time. And although I never sensed it had much to do with me or the family, I *felt* it, the sadness.

Four decades later, I would begin to understand. In the process of early recovery from alcoholism and bulimia, the sadness would return and, slowly, its origin and meanings would begin to unfold. With the help of twelve-step recovery, a strong network of friends, and an abundance of resources for healing and liberation that I have encountered through study, teaching, and writing, play, spiritual searching, emotional and political work, I began to see that the "cloud" hanging over me as a child was *class injury*. By class injury, I mean an amorphous blend of economic fear, insecurity, and shame that permeated middle-class U.S. cultures in the mid-twentieth century and still does today, taking different shapes among various racial, ethnic, and religious groups. I began to understand this cloud and sadness *not* as an emotional problem that belonged uniquely to either my family or me but rather as a sign of our radical alienation—that is, a social, economic, and political problem that truly mystifies the emotional, spiritual, and physical well-being of all segments of our society. I'm referring to life in this Western society, although alienation is a global problem shaped differently from one context to another. For example, as a structure of alienation, sexism looks different in China, the

United States, Saudi Arabia, and South Africa, but sexism permeates these and other nations.

Alienation is not, at root, a feeling.[1] It is a primary consequence of unjust power relations in which particular groups of people are held systematically over other groups—white, economically privileged people, for example, over others, alienated from others and others from us. Often we do not feel alienated at all—we do not feel anything. And this is part of the problem, for we have learned not to notice our alienation. Yet all the while it is doing to our psyches—to our capacities for love and work—what polluted air is doing to our bodies. It is wearing us down and, over time, silencing, separating, and shattering us, collectively and individually.

As sin, alienation is not simply a state of psychospiritual estrangement from God, though it is also that, which is how Tillich and others have grasped and articulated the psychospiritual condition that is both a cause and consequence of modern patterns of alienation (one pattern being the exploitative character of advanced capitalism).[2] As a liberation theologian, I am interested in economic, racial, sexual, and other patterns into which we are born and in which our psychospiritualities are being shaped probably *in utero* and surely within the first hours and days of our lives on planet earth. We are, in this sense, born alienated, born into Augustine's *massa damnata* and original sin, not because our parents lusted after each other but because they, too, our families of origin and of adoption, our communities, and our cultures, have been and are alienated, "living in sin."

Let me press on a bit into this "damned mass" that is our common problem and is connected with *all* mental and emotional problems, whatever their biochemical or personal/familial sources. In a profit-consumed economic order, the value of persons, collectively and individually, is diminished. The accumulation of capital on the part of the wealthy and the hope for wealth on the part of the rest of us in Western society are designed to take precedence over the essentially nonmonetary value of human beings and other earth creatures as significant and worthy simply because we are who we are. In this context, the capacity to love and respect our bodies, enjoy a strong sense of self-esteem, take real pleasure in our work, and respect and enjoy others is always a weakened capacity. We have to struggle for it. In a literal sense, even before we individually "get here," we have lost ourselves as a people in solidarity with one another and other creatures. If we are lucky—by birth, adoption, and/or community—we begin as children and continue into our adulthood and throughout our lives struggling for right—mutually empowering, unalienated—power relations: struggling to "re-member" ourselves, to put back together a solidarity with one another that has been lost, a vision we share that historically eludes us, collectively and individually.

Now, this loss of ourselves and one another—this condition into which we are born—is what Karl Marx meant by "alienation."[3] It forms the basis for what psychiatrist and Stone Center research director Jean Baker Miller names as our "disconnections," the "intensely cofounded opposites of the 'good things' that flow from growth-enhancing, mutually empowering connections,"[4] mutually empowering relationships being those in which *all* of us are being called forth to be ourselves at our best. "Alienation" is the political and psychosocial door through which adolescent girls pass, losing their voice, as Carol Gilligan, Annie Rogers, and their feminist colleagues at the Harvard School of Education have suggested.[5] In an alienated situation, no one relates as humanely as she or he might wish. It is not that we individually do not want to be caring people, not that we do not want to experience and share the "good things" that flow from mutually empowering relationship. It is rather that largely unbeknownst to us in the course of living our daily lives, we are being shaped by social forces that literally are generating our feelings and values. In this situation, the ability to affect anything much, the power to make a difference, means *power over* others, power to *control* others as well as ourselves.

Note here the dualistic concept of "self"—split theologically and morally as well as psychologically—between a higher (in control) and lower (out of control) self. This split, with its modern ring, echoes, of course, the classic christian split between Spirit and Body. The objectification of ourselves, and alienation from our bodyselves, is hardly a new development. It didn't arrive with global capitalism or with modern technology, but these forces are shaping it. In an alienated situation, "power" means domination, however unconscious, by a few over the lives and deaths of many. I refer here to the real, daily control—the naming, distribution, or withholding—of all human and other natural resources such as the food we eat, the air we breathe, the energy we burn, and the love we make. Even the dreams we nurture today in Western society are controlled to a large extent by the interests of affluent white males who usually fail to see the exploitative character of their own lives. That is to say, most men are not, individually, "bad" men. Like most women, most men don't have a clue that they are playing social roles into which they have been cast. Men and women alike assume that our roles are "natural." This is an assumption upon which we work and love, fear and hope, and it is a radical misperception—this sense that our alienation is simply "the way it is" and that our healing in this context means getting "adjusted" to, even comfortable with, the situation.

I believe the work of psychospiritual healing—pastoral care—can be understood, practiced, and experienced as a resource for resistance to alienation. It should be a resource in our struggle against forces of alienated power that silence, separate, and shatter us collectively and individually—forces like sexism (male gender entitlement), racism (white cultural, economic, and political supremacy), and heterosexism (a logical, necessary extension of sexism, in which "manhood" is synonymous with men's control of women's bodies and desires).[6]

Let me elaborate briefly on classism,[7] one of the most difficult structures of alienated power for us in the United States to recognize. Classism makes fools of us, teaching us to imagine that self-worth can be bought if we try harder. What might we learn together in our seminaries and churches about our lives in relation to forces of economic power, privilege, and class injury if we were to risk moving through our fear and shame by beginning to share and study the meanings of our "money" stories, our stories of pride and fear, of insecurity and shame, of aspiration and confusion?

I believe that, if we were to take this seriously as basic to theological, and christian, education, we would begin to make connections between class, our own histories, our communities, and our experiences and understandings of God. We would begin to make connections across race and ethnic lines, across class and religion, across national and cultural histories. We in Western cultures would discover that all of us have been injured by class dynamics in late capitalism, though not always in the same ways, and that all of our various emotional and mental problems—and the problems of those with whom we work pastorally—have been, to some degree, shaped and exacerbated by class injury—such as the "cloud" which hung over a childhood that was otherwise relatively happy, safe, and secure.

Moreover, we would begin to see, through intuition as well as cognition, that the "god-images" presented through theological discourse are shaped, to significant degrees, by class. Consider, for example, Karl Barth's faith in a "Wholly Other God"[8] and Delores Williams's in the power that sustained Hagar the slave woman in the wilderness.[9] These god-images reflect different class experiences.

For Barth, an anthropomorphic (but distinctly other) God

speaks, reaches, and gives to all humanity, but we cannot receive or respond unless, by the grace and power of God in
Christ, we let go entirely of our worldly agendas and material desires. For Williams, there may be no wholly other or
anthropomorphized deity acting on behalf of African American women. Rather, generations of black women have struggled for survival on the basis of their belief that their Lord
Jesus is with them specifically in their agenda, as black
women, not to let go of their embodied, material commitment to the survival of their people. These are not "right"
and "wrong" theologies, but they represent very different
human experiences and understandings of how the source of
life itself is connected to money, worldly power, and material privilege. As such, they suggest very different contexts
and opportunities for pastoral ministry.

It is not within the scope of this essay to elaborate on how
particular theological traditions, such as neo-orthodoxy and
womanism, do or do not help some of us and not others pastorally. It is important, however, for us to realize that different theological traditions often can help us in different ways
and in different areas of our work. It is important also for us
to see that some theological sources, traditions, and images
will help us *more* than others, depending on who we are, on
the particular contexts of our pastoral commitments, and on
how particular theologies do or do not help us connect with
our people and with other parts of creation—animals, plants,
earth. It is also immensely important for us to realize that *all*
theologies, psychologies, and other theoretical constructs—
whether or not their authors acknowledge it (and most white
men do not)—are shaped by particular class, race, gender,
and other socio-political experiences and interests.

The rest of this essay will be an attempt to illustrate how
hetero/sexism, racism, classism, and other structures of
alienated power are basic issues for any pastoral care and
theology.

RESISTANCE TO ALIENATION:
BASIS OF PASTORAL CARE

You may know the work of Audre Lorde, renowned poet, activist, and lesbian feminist theorist. Addressing another African American woman who had agreed to be her therapist, Lorde wrote:

Dear Leora,

For two Black women to enter an analytic or therapeutic relationship means beginning an essentially uncharted and insecure journey. There are no prototypes, no models, no objectively accessible body of experience other than ourselves by which to examine the specific dynamics of our interaction as Black women. Yet this interaction can affect all the other psychic matter attended profoundly. It is to scrutinize that very interaction that I sought you out professionally, and I have come to see that it means picking our way through our similarities and our differences, as well as through our histories of calculated mistrust and desire. . . .

The territory between us feels new and frightening as well as urgent, rigged with detonating pieces of our own individual racial histories which neither of us chose but which each of us bears the scars from. And those are particular to each of us. But there is a history which we share because we are Black women in a racist sexist cauldron, and that means some part of this journey is yours, also. . . .

We have only who we are, with or without the courage to use those selves for further exploration and clarification of how what lies between us as Black women affects us and the work we do together. . . .

If we do not do it here between us, each one of us will have to do it somewhere else, sometime.

I know these things: I do not yet know what to do about them. But I do want to make them fit together to serve my life and my work, and I don't mean merely in a way that feels safe. I don't know how they can further illuminate your life and work, but I know they can....

I look forward to our meeting eye to eye.

Audre[10]

Several therapists, responding to this letter, have remarked that this is not a typical patient. "There aren't many Audre Lordes in therapy!" one woman exclaimed. I'm painfully aware that there aren't many women in our society with such psychological strength and self-confidence. The forces of alienated power have seen to that. Indeed, there aren't, in that sense, many "Audre Lordes" in, or out, of psychotherapy. But it is my experience that those students and others who turn to me professionally when they are in pain or crisis respond in positive ways when I *expect* them to meet me as sisters or brothers who share with me a stake in how the world turns out and whose pain, whatever its source, I understand to be in basic ways a pain that belongs to all. And so, while there aren't many Audre Lordes in the world that white privileged men have constructed, this is no accident. And there will be more strong, self-confident, justice-seeking, compassionate people to the extent that we, in our work, *expect* folks to discover, recover, and celebrate themselves and meet us mutually as sisters and brothers.

I offer an example of a mutually empowering dynamic in a pastoral relationship that took place in my life more than twenty years ago. My relationship with my pastoral psychotherapist Christopher (pseudonym), a white heterosexual man, was remarkable in its holding of our capacities for a mutuality that would unfold slowly over the four-year period of therapy. During this time, I was struggling with my sexuality—was I, or was I not, homosexual? bisexual? (I would never have used the term "lesbian" in those days. It was too loaded, sexually and politically.) When I first mentioned my confusion about my sexuality, Christopher told me that this made him anxious and that his anxiety was *his* problem, *not mine.* He wanted me to know this, he said, because I would surely pick up the anxiety in the room and it would be important for me to realize that *I* was doing nothing wrong.

Four years later, at the end of our work together as therapist and client, as we moved toward a collegial friendship, Christopher told me how he had been changed through our work. Looking back, as a lesbian, I cannot imagine a better relational environment within which to have worked on the disorder of heterosexism and disease of homophobia—that of others, and my own internalized stuff—than in relationship to someone who was homophobic, who knew it and said so, who acknowledged it as his own problem, and who let the force of our relationship touch and change his consciousness, politics, and the way he practices therapy to this day.

Since 1987, I've been collaborating with Janet Surrey, a white feminist, clinical psychologist, and research associate of the Stone Center at Wellesley College, on our shared interest in *mutuality.* Together with others involved in healing work—especially women in recovery; women making connections, cross-culturally, between social forces and their own lives; and women (clients and therapists) who have been wounded in psychotherapy—Jan and I have come to understand more clearly that mutuality is *relational movement,* not a static way of being. It is a dynamic process generated by a shared assumption that all parties in a relationship can, and should, be empowered through the relational process.

From an ethical perspective, mutuality is the creative response to alienated power and offers our only hope for transforming alienated power into an energy for making justice. In the context of alienated power, mutuality means struggling against the forces that silence, separate, and shatter us. The ongoingness of the struggle against these forces is what keeps our visions of mutuality from being sentimental ideals that cannot be realized.

Relational mutuality requires first then a commitment to struggling for it. This is what gives relational psychology its moral or ethical foundation. This commitment is seasoned in visions, experiences, and intimations of the intrinsically relational character of who we are. White feminist psychologist Brinton Lykes speaks of our "social individuality,"[11] much as the Stone Center has written about our "mutual growth in connection."[12] Jewish existentialist and social philosopher Martin Buber described the sacred power working in the "in-between."[13] Vietnamese poet and teacher Thich Nhat Hahn bears witness to a life force that connects all created beings.[14] But actually to feel this life force, this moral and psychological foundation—to experience it as "empathy," "compassion," or "love"—requires first that we be committed to struggling for it as the basis of our lives.

Genuine mutuality emerges only then, out of this struggle, as a shared capacity to experience our voices although we have been silenced; our connectedness although we have been separated; and our integrity as persons although we have been shattered. These destructive effects of alienation have taken especially high tolls on the lives of women, children, and marginalized men.

Up to this point, I have been writing largely in nongender-specific ways of our alienation and our pastoral work of resistance and mutuality, understanding that how we experience alienation and how we may work most creatively varies considerably, given differences among us of race, class, gender, sexuality, age, abilities, and religious/theological traditions. From this point on, I will be writing more specifically about *women's* lives as pastoral context and more self-consciously as a woman involved in teaching, sacramental, and social action ministries. Men are invited to read for what these women's lives, and my words, may be suggesting about your lives and your pastoral work as our brothers in the struggle.

I want to suggest to my sisters that our pastoral care (especially, though not only, with women, children, and marginalized men) should be opening us and those who seek our help to three ongoing relational processes:

1. We should be listening to many different voices.
2. We should be making intimate connections with one another.
3. We should be experiencing a seasoning of personal integrity, our own and in others.

As pastors, we should be listening to, offering access to, and evoking many different voices.[15] As Nelle Morton so powerfully spoke, we must "hear each other to speech."[16] That is pastoral work, and it is critical in a culture of alienation that has silenced so many of us, especially women, through sexual and other forms of violence.

Over the last ten years, as you know, much psychotherapy has been empowering for many "survivors" of sexual abuse.[17] I'm sure many of you have been doing this important work, as therapists, pastors, and those seeking help. And the pastoral work of healing is not only to help us survive but also to empower us to thrive as resisters, which, for all of us, involves learning to hear and heed our own and others' creative, liberating voices. Breaking the silence forced upon us by generations of sexual, racial, class, religious, domestic, and other forms of abuse requires our learning to hear and respect the voices of those whose experiences of abuse and healing may be different from our own. Let me give you an example of a woman whose experiences are different in some significant ways from many of ours.

Ruth (pseudonym) is an African American friend of mine

in her late forties. She had a middle-class upbringing in the North with her mother who was a secretary and father who, born and raised as a sharecropper, worked as a grocer. The eldest of three children and the only girl, Ruth was raped by her father through much of her childhood and early teens. Today, as a physician, Ruth spends much time with other women who have been hurt, sexually and otherwise, as girls or women and whose healing requires, in every case, that they explore their pain and come to understand through it, through multi-focal lenses of an alienation that is never simply sexual but always is shaped by such forces as racism and race privilege, class privilege, class injury, anti-Semitism, sexism, heterosexism, and so forth.

In Ruth's case, her healing from the wound of incest involved her being a primary caretaker for her father during the last two years of his life as he died of cancer. Did she feel conflicted? Yes. Was she angry? Yes. Did she want to be caring for this man? *Yes—and no.* Ruth's healing required friends and a therapist who knew that the relationship between Ruth and her father—the incest as well as her caring for him later in his life—was shaped by interweaving forces of how both father and daughter experienced racism, being a black family in racist America, class injury and cross-generational class confusion (father and daughter "moving up" in terms of socio-economic status, but at different times and in different ways), and, of course, the relative nature of black male gender privilege in white racist society. As Ruth points out, these power dynamics shifted dramatically as she grew up and rose professionally above her own father. She reminded me, as I prepared this presentation, that relational power—between parents and children—often changes over time, as it did in her case.

Unlike those who feel they must disconnect from those who have violated them, Ruth's situation enabled her to stay connected with her father. The shift in socio-economic power and self-esteem between her father and herself—her ability to meet her father as his social and personal peer—enabled her to stand with her father through his illness and death. Ruth's story suggests that, when we are empowered relationally, we have a greater range of options from which to make relational choices. Moreover, we may see that Ruth's capacity for compassion—which she cultivated through friendship, womanist politics, strong faith in a god of justice, professional work, therapy with a sister who was learning and growing with her, and her relationship with her father—became a well-spring of her healing and a basis of her desire for connection with others.

Be clear. This was not, and is not, a matter simply of "forgiving and forgetting." If Ruth's story is to be heard at all as a story of forgiveness, it should help us see that Ruth's capacity to forgive—that is, to break the stranglehold the past might have held on her life—required a strong sisterly and brotherly network of helpers, folks holding her up, learning with her dynamics of healing and liberation. Throughout the most intensive period of Ruth's healing, as her father was dying, Ruth's therapist was struggling with her to understand a complex of power dynamics, emotions, and insights that had as much to teach the therapist—a white, middle-class woman—about violence, trauma, and compassion as they did Ruth.

Ruth agrees that it was a multiplicity of *voices* in her life that enabled her healing: her own voices and those of others, including her father, her therapist, her friends, artists, authors, and poets; the more political voices and the more psychological; the more personal voices and the more professional; the more intuitive voices and the more analytical; the angrier voices and the more confused; unforgiving voices and compassionate voices; African American voices, Anglo voices, feminist and womanist voices.

What might we learn from Ruth's experience—from what she learned? What would it mean for our pastoral work *routinely* to involve our listening to different voices from within, among, and around us?

Consider for a moment what we might learn from one of the most interesting phenomena in our midst today—the presence of many persons who are divided internally into different "persons" and different "voices." This "dissociation" is a remarkably creative way that many children and adults, especially women, unconsciously have devised to cope with trauma (usually some terrible violence in childhood). Women and men suffering from dissociative disorders have much, I believe, to teach us about our fear of hearing "different voices" and about the courage required to confront, and learn from, difference.

Lesbian feminist psychiatrist Peggy Hanley-Hackenbruck points out that the problem in a multiple personality disorder (MPD) is not the multiplicity of voices but rather their inability to communicate.[18] Canadian feminist psychologist Margo Rivera says that the problem most therapists have in treating MPD, even those who strongly accept it as a dissociative phenomenon, is that they themselves are so afraid of it.[19]

In learning from students with dissociative experiences—ranging from significant memory lapses to experiences of having multiple personalities—and on the assumption that we're all dissociated to some extent simply to cope in a violent world, I've come to believe that we usually are afraid of hearing too many voices within us or around us; afraid we will be unable to communicate with the different "personalities," persons, groups, opinions, ideologies; afraid we will be overwhelmed, further silenced, perhaps shattered, if we are faced with too much conflict, argument, disagreement, or differences of perspective.

But we know today, in education and theology, that we continually are having to revamp our courses and curricula to be more responsive to the legitimate, radical claims of different constituencies. To teach theology in the late twentieth century is no longer to read and discuss books written by one race and one gender. It is to give white men their own, more modest, places in theological curricula that are no longer and never again will be monologues of Western men's opinions. The best curricula are becoming roundtable discussions— ever-expanding in shape, multi-colored and cultured in voices. How might we in our pastoral work be learning, hearing, experiences and perspectives—voices within, between, and around us all? How can we cultivate the courage to participate in processes of learning and healing that will move us beyond the symbolic universes set in place by Western men and their disciples?

Our pastoral work should be opening us and others with us to multiplicities of voices, stories, and interpretations as resources for healing and liberation.

Our pastoral work also should be helping us make significant, intimate connections with others—making trustworthy, non-abusive, mutual connection where we have been separated and divided by structures of alienation, such as classism.

Let me give two troubling examples from psychotherapy. One of my students, Nelle (pseudonym)—a divorced white woman with working-class roots who was in school part-time and holding down a full-time job to support herself and daughter—was told by her black female therapist that her difficulties in paying for therapy signaled her "resistance to treatment." When Nelle asked that they at least talk about money matters, the therapist suggested they do it the following week. When Nelle arrived for therapy the following week, the therapist told her that this would be their final session and proceeded to terminate the therapy. More than a decade later, Nelle still cannot recount this experience without crying.

Another white student, Martha (pseudonym), who as a child had been sexually molested by her upper-class, exceedingly prominent father, wished to explore with her therapist and her therapy group (all white women) ways in which the class and race privilege of her family not only had shaped her experience of sexual violation but also had contributed to how her mother had dealt with what was happening in the family—for example, through the denial she believed would protect the family name and, ironically, her daughter's "honor." When it seemed to Martha that her therapist and other group members weren't especially interested in these issues and seemed, in fact, to believe they were getting the therapy "off-track," Martha dropped out of the group and out of therapy.

What seems to me especially important about what happened between Nelle, Martha, and their respective therapists is that injuries of class separated woman from woman. Classism is alienation that pervades our lives. How we understand pastoral care to some degree will mirror how class realities and injuries have shaped our experiences of work, love, healing, spirituality, and other dimensions of our lives that bear directly upon our work as pastors.

I'd venture to guess that most pastoral care givers, like most therapists, don't talk much about money with those who seek their help. This is more or less true of most of us. We refuse to engage one another about money matters. We meet each other in silence and avoidance. We don't see what, if anything, money and class have to do, basically, with psychospiritual growth or theological education. We are silenced and, in effect, separated by this structure of alienation because class functions more or less invisibly among us. We learn to believe it really doesn't matter too much, that we really don't need to understand it in order to understand ourselves, one another, or the Spirit that connects us. In our silence, we cultivate class ignorance which becomes increasingly basic to how we live and work and to what we see and choose not to see about ourselves, the world, God, and those who seek our help.

In addition to the invisibility of class and our ignorance about it, class separates us because we fear the intimacy of so vulnerably knowing and being known by others. Nothing, including sex, is more difficult for most of us to discuss honestly with others than how we really feel about ourselves and others in relation to matters of class. There is, I believe, no more basic pastoral work than to help women, men, and children deal honestly with injuries of class, which means that care givers must be honest about these injuries in their own lives. And it is, of course, important for pastors and therapists to realize that nothing, including sexual abuse, has done more across lines of race and culture to diminish women's (and men's) senses of self-worth and confidence. Pastoral care is, after all, about building our capacities for intimacy and mutuality in a world in which we have been separated and isolated from one another by such all-pervasive forces as class injury.

As pastors, we and those with whom we work, should be seeking greater personal integrity, seeking to be less at odds with ourselves, more humane and compassionate with others. In the context of the alienation that shatters us, leaving us broken, feeling fragmented and crazy, our pastoral need—and our need as pastors—is to be people with integrity, involved in a lifetime journey of making right relation with one another and with the whole created earth. It is an ongoing process. We are participants in it. That is the root of our integrity as persons, our "wholeness." Pastoral ministry should be a resource in which we are discovering together that our integrity is seasoned in the struggles for mutuality, justice, and compassion. Our psychospiritual well-being will never be a matter of getting it all together, of recovering completely, of getting beyond a need for help. Our psychospiritual integrity enables us to rest assured that our personal well-being will always be rooted in our interest in, and solidarity with, others.

Let me give an example of a woman's struggle for personal well-being and integrity.

Page (pseudonym) is a white woman in her early 60s, married, mother of two sons, activist for many years on behalf of women's lives, especially poor women in this and other countries. Six or seven years ago, Page began to talk with some of her friends and colleagues about her childhood experience of having been raped by her father who was a well-known, liberal protestant pastor, himself the son of an even better-known clergyman. Through the years that Page and her siblings were being raped by their father, he was beating, brutalizing, and raping his wife.

When his wife, Page's mother, went to the bishop to tell him what was happening in their home, the bishop told her to go home and try to be a "forgiving" wife. "Otherwise," he said, "you'll ruin a good pastor." (This will sound familiar to those who have been following reports of how church authorities historically have dealt with sexual abuse by clergy.) Shortly thereafter, Page's mother was committed to a mental hospital where she spent the next twenty years. She was released several years before she died as a poor woman with little more than the clothes on her back and her daughter's love.

Being a teacher, pastor, and friend to Page through her process of healing has been a profoundly moving experience for me. Through her therapy, her work with poor and other abused women, her deep involvement in—and, eventually, departure from—the church, and her feminist spirituality and politics, Page emerged as a spokeswoman for and champion of women abused in the church—not only by its clergy but also by its sexist/heterosexist theology, rituals, and tradition. With many other women, Page views christian tradition itself as abusive, a tradition that invites men to behave like her father. As a christian priest, I believe she is right.

Page has become increasingly aware that her integrity as a

person is an unending process being shaped in the struggles for justice, compassion, and mutuality, whether in family or church, in movements for reproductive rights or for victims' rights, in Boston or San Salvador, Haiti, South Africa, or South Korea. She has lamented with her sisters how hard it was to find a therapist who could walk this way with her, as a sister committed to the claims of liberation as the spark of personal integrity.

Our integrity is rooted in right relation. It enables us to honor and respect different voices, to struggle through our fears of difference and intimacy, to take the risks involved in being ourselves, in letting ourselves be known. In these times, we need to nuance and modify our insistence upon professional "boundaries" and "safety" with an equally strong pastoral commitment to right—mutually empowering—relation throughout our lives, including our professional work.[20] A strong sisterly or brotherly love, mutually respectful and caring, is the basis of all healing, liberation, and pastoral work. Mutual relation is *de facto* nonviolent and nonabusive, because it is a way of honoring differences (including differences in power), a way of respecting bodily integrity, a way of taking seriously our shared need not to be manipulated, disregarded, or discarded by anyone.

Feminist scholar and teacher Donna Haraway, a historian of biology whose primary area of research has been with primates, suggests that the only chance we have for a future is learning how to live in the radical relativity—relationality—of our lives, with and amidst our different cultures, languages, and systems of meaning. We do not need, nor will we ever have, a "common language," Haraway writes. If we are to have a chance for the future, what we need, she suggests, describes beautifully a goal and vision for pastoral work: to make "no-nonsense commitments [to a world] that can be partially shared and friendly to earth-wide projects of finite freedom, adequate material abundance, modest meaning in suffering, and limited happiness."[21]

Without such a radically social basis, I believe our pastoral work has no moral basis at all. Of course, it is not easy to imagine how to live and work in this way. It is always harder to be ethical, caring people than simply to do what we are told.[22] But, if we share such a commitment and are willing to struggle together toward what we envision, the paths will be opened to us and we will find ourselves and one another, sisters and brothers, along the way. For as a beautiful sister reminds us, "the journey is home."[23]

PART 3

Re-Imagining

One of the things I try to keep in mind as I teach is that, regardless of how inclusive we think we're being at any moment of our theological work, we're always leaving someone out. I insist to my students that we need always be asking, "Who are we leaving out?" or "Who is not here, and why?" and really wrestle for answers to these important theological and ethical questions.

11

Turning to the Animals
Another Conversion

Sometime ago a bear made its way over the bridge that connects the mainland to the island off the Maine coast where I spend much of my summer. Word went out and excitement spread among the men and boys. Within three hours, they say, that bear was hanging dead in a public place. This story circulated during the summer among folks on the island. Each teller spoke with a mixture of sadness and anger, but no one was in the least surprised. "That's just the way it is," a woman sighed; "if it's different, men kill it."

The problem as I see it is not simply the gratuitous killing of one more earth creature, though that is a moral problem that should raise ethical questions for us. The larger picture is that this event exemplifies a ritual of boys being boys or, worse, of boys becoming men and of men simply being themselves in a culture that teaches and preaches domination and conquest as a way of life for "real [white] men."

Be clear that men of color and women are not exempt from responsibility in perpetuating this culture of death, but our violent acts tend often to be twisted, self-defeating efforts to get along, even survive, in hetero/sexist racist patriarchy. This doesn't make us more innocent than our white brothers or morally superior to them; it does mean we're less likely than white men to survive even the effects of our own violence, much less thrive in a society in which women and children of all colors and men of color, historically and habitually, are slaughtered—like the bear—when we dare to cross into white men's turf.

Isn't this really also the story of a black man chased down and murdered on New York's Howard Beach because he was "just" a black man and of a gay sailor mutilated by a shipmate in a men's room in Japan because he was "just" a homosexual? The story of a woman raped, beaten, and left for dead in Central Park because she was "just" a woman; of a little girl in Maine cooked in her mother's oven because she was "just" a child; and of pelicans crucified on pieces of wood in California because they were "just" birds? This dreadful story is about a bear, yes, and it is also about Wounded Knee and Treblinka and Soweto and Sarajevo, about earth creatures destroyed because they were "just" Indians, or Jews, or blacks, or Muslims.

The story is not about hunting to survive or even simply about reckless, deadly play. It's about killing to secure one's membership in a dominant species, a "sport" we've learned to tolerate even when we demur, as best we can, from active participation. I wonder if we trivialize by turning away from the fate of nonhuman animals *not* because we don't think it's important but because we *know* it's all connected, the bear and Bosnia, and we simply are overwhelmed. What to do in this ghastly, violent situation? Here I am exploring a few theological reasons why christians ought to do something about the culture of violence and death that our own religious tradition has helped put in place and to make a few suggestions as to what to do about it.

HOW WE EXPERIENCE THE WORLD

Feminist liberation theologians understand that we can speak truthfully about God only insofar as we are speaking truthfully about how we experience the world. It's not that God is synonymous with the world but rather that we *know* God through our embodied, daily experiences in and of the world. Regardless of our particular church tradition, however, most christians have been weaned on the contrary assumption that we are closest to the creator when we are farthest away from the creation, lifted above ourselves.

H. Paul Santmire names this latter assumption the "motif of ascent" in christianity and acknowledges that it signals the most common christian response to the creation: the effort to rise above it through prayer, denial, and, in effect, through neglect and indifference.[1] Santmire suggests that there is another, less evident, but more morally forceful motif in christian history—an "ecological" theme—that meets us through not only Francis of Assisi at the turn of the thirteenth century and other creation-loving individuals but much earlier in the works of Augustine, fourth- and fifth-century bishop of Hippo; Irenaeus, second-century bishop of Lyons; and in "the dynamics of Hebraic faith, the proclamation of Jesus, and the theology of Paul and the Pauline authors of Colossians and Ephesians,"[2] in which the *whole* creation, not just its human component, is celebrated as God's own.

While I appreciate Santmire's perception that there is a creation-affirming thread that runs through christianity (and he invites us to look for it in places many feminists are cautious about—e.g., Augustine, Luther, and Calvin!), Santmire does not name as *morally* problematic the *most ecologically devastating* motif in christianity and Judaism—and that is the *domination* motif that pushes its way through the history, especially, of the followers of Jesus.

Domination is the problem that feminist and gay liberation ethical-theologians such as Rosemary Radford Ruether, Sallie McFague, J. Michael Clark, and Daniel Spencer[3] cite as foundational to the problems the church has always had with nonhuman nature as well as with our own embodied, human, selves—especially *female* body and selves. Santmire, like the majority of men and women of good will who are concerned about how christians act in relation to the creation, does not seem to notice the fundamental connection between how the church has treated *women, sex, and bodies* and how it views the *nonhuman members of creation*—Bosnia and the bear.

The connection is christian complicity in and identification with patterns of *domination*. This connection is thoroughly entangled with the roots of christianity's positioning of its god above the world, its christ isolated as a male savior above and in opposition to history, its church above nonchristian people, its men above women and children, and its people above nonhuman creatures. It is a matter of how we experience the world in terms of who owns whom and of who is entitled—who is spiritually authorized, called by God—to control whom. Feminist liberation theologians suggest that women's lives and embodied selves bear witness to the answer to this question. Depending upon the circumstances of our lives, we may in our own times and places experience the world as full of wonder and joy but, if we are honest with ourselves in relation to our sister and brother earth creatures, human and other, we also experience the world shattered by violence—violence aimed at everyone, but justified as right or appropriate when women, children, and nonhuman creatures are the victims. And this experience of violence, and of the despair it calls forth, evokes our prayer and generates our spirituality.

This is why feminist, gay, lesbian, and other liberation theologians insist in our work that, if we are to speak of God at all, we must be raising questions about economic exploitation of all creatures in late monopoly capitalism as it advances globally and about the interactive design of white racism and male gender oppression and compulsory heterosexuality and christianity's claim, implicit or explicit, to possess spiritually the final, supreme, religious truth. Feminist liberation theology must insist that we dig vigorously and patiently for roots that connect what happened to the bear and what happens constantly to human and nonhuman earth creatures in a world in which the dominant patriarchal religions, especially christianity, have taught us to control—or, if we must, destroy—that which is sensual, embodied, down-to-earth, womanly, childlike, and those creaturely impulses (e.g., sexual desire) that turn us away from "spiritual" things.

As far as we humans can tell, time is not on "our side" in relation to the survival of life, human and other, on this planet. What might this fundamental ethical and pastoral challenge suggest to us as earth creatures, whether or not we are christian?

TURNING TO THE ANIMALS

For all of our history as "civilized" man and, certainly, as "christian soldiers," we have turned to a god whom we believe is Lord and Father of all. From time to time, folks have come along with other images of the Sacred and at times we have tolerated them—Francis of Assisi comes to mind, and other prophets and poets and political revolutionaries and peacemakers—as long as their challenges to the patriarchal foundations of christianity do not threaten actually to transform it. But, I believe, with other feminist liberation theologians on every continent of our planet home today, that christianity *must* be transformed, its patriarchal assumptions uprooted, its symbolic universe reimaged, if we are to bear life and hope in and for the world rather than continue to help hold in place the cultures of death and despair we have helped create.

But where and how in the world do we even begin such spiritual work? Maybe, in the tradition of religious conversion—of "turning around"—we should turn in a new direction. Maybe we should turn to the animals rather than the heavens—not to the animals of our idealized imaginations, not to the "peaceable kingdom," not to our fantasized notions of beasts who do no harm to one another "except for food," but rather to the real world of animals if we really hope to meet and be met by our salvation. What might we learn, we christians, from the animals?

Three lessons for starters, I believe: (1) something about the sacredness of otherness that we, as *christians*, have not known; (2) something about justice that we as *western* christians have not understood very well; and (3) something about the radicalness and extent of incarnation that we as *humans* have not been encouraged, through patriarchal religion, to realize.

1. Sacred Other

Much of our christian heritage has been steeped in an assumption that God is indeed "other" than us: that is, we are *not* God. Although through the living presence of Jesus, we may experience the Sacred as *with* us—Spirit-guide, Higher Power, liberator, friend—God is essentially "other" than human and very definitely "other" than bear or lizard or snail. The term used by christian theologians for this "otherness" has been "transcendence":[4] God may be with us, but God is also "somewhere else." God may be like us, but God is also unlike us. Most, if not all, christians over the two millennia of the church have assumed, moreover, that God is *more* "like" us, even in His [sic] otherness, than "like" a whale, much less a serpent. Perhaps even Jesus, our brother from Nazareth, was inclined to experience his human friends as more "important" to God than sparrows. But might we faithfully assume, like us, Jesus had much to learn about the world of God?

We as christians, and here I speak especially of we who are white western christians with our human-centered—anthropocentric and, therefore, anthropomorphic—faith, have not learned to see images of God in "other" members of creation, the slugs and sharks we often try to avoid as well as the dogs and dolphins whose company we seek. Having learned that we humans are the only creatures with "soul," "conscience," or "morals," we have disregarded the actual basis of all authentic morality, which is the making of right-relation with the whole created world in all of its otherness and differences from us.

Turning to the animals, we are called to reckon with the blasphemy of the hunt for sport and to consider seriously what it means for us to eat cows and chickens and fish raised in a spirit of indifference to their suffering in order to maximize our profit and pleasure. I do not believe it is ethical for us to eat animals—and I have not yet given up this practice entirely. I think we should be considering this matter collectively, as church communities, wrestling with it as a serious moral question and not be torn between our pangs of conscience and our sense that it really doesn't make much difference to the animals or anyone else what we do individually.

At the very least, every christian man, woman, and child —if we raise or eat meat—should be doing so with a great deal of humility and gratitude to the animals themselves and, through them, to the One who gives herself or himself so that we may live: *"Take, eat. Is this not my body?"*

2. Justice as Mutual Relation
Justice making is the on-going movement to create right, mutually empowering relation by which all persons or parties are accorded respect and basic resources for quality of life.[5] Justice making requires more than our effort to achieve "equality" between different genders, races, or other groups. I believe we must struggle toward extending our understandings of justice to include taking seriously, not romanticizing, our mutuality with animals and the earth. That most of us do not know how to do this or what it may involve says to me that we have much to learn.

Certainly, it is important, simply for sake of compassion and decency, that we learn to treat our animal companions on the earth with much greater kindness and respect than we, collectively, have thought much about. Turning to the animals, we may be led to see that a justice-centered theory of "animal rights"—and that is what is called for—is not simply about keeping chickens in cleaner coops, although it includes this commitment. Justice making must also be about tearing down the material, ideological, and spiritual boundaries that prevent us from realizing, and creating together, the conditions that will enable us to live—and eat—in a spirit of more genuine mutuality with other human beings and with animals.

By "boundaries," I am referring to social, religious, economic, and other institutions and structures that promote domination and control as the basis of our life together; systems and ways of organizing our lives that keep us from realizing deep in our selves that we frogs and elephants and humans are an ecosystem of blood and tears and hunger and growth and disease and possibility and that whether we like one another or not, or whether we see any "reason" for one another or not, we *need* one another. We need one another not only because we are members of the same ecosystem but also because we are different. Justice, as mutually empowering relation, is possible *because* we are different. It requires us to respect and honor one another in our differences.

Justice demands that we see, in the bear, not an image of ourselves (what Teilhard de Chardin and many other christians who attempt to take creation seriously tend to assume), but rather an image of a *bear*, and that we *welcome* the bear not as we might greet a human sister or brother but rather as we should greet a sister or brother *bear*. That we perhaps cannot imagine what this means, much less how to do it, except with guns, is not surprising given the scarcity of ethical resources we, as western, Eurocentric christians, bring to the possibility of celebrating mutuality with either human or nonhuman creatures.

We need practice! We need to be helping one another learn how we really might turn to the animals—*including the humans most vulnerable to the ravages of violence*—in order to learn what we need to learn from those that are different from us, those most alien. Just as we white christians need to be listening to people of color and nonchristians, we humans need to be listening to pigs and porcupines and mudflats and rivers with an attentiveness that allows us to learn from "others"— be they bluefish or trees. The church has a responsibility— theologically and ethically, pastorally and liturgically—to help us learn how to envision, create, and live together in right relation on this planet.

3. Come. The spirit of the women burnt . . . the rain forest murdered . . . the earth, air, and water, raped[6]
Early in 1991, Korean feminist theologian Chung Hyun Kyung spoke to the World Council of Churches meeting in Canberra. In her talk, Chung called forth the spirit of women, men, and other creatures, invoking the presence of the power that moves through and infuses the many dimensions of the universe. Chung was bearing witness to a shamanistic tradition that takes seriously the sacred, godly presence in and of all living things.

A storm of controversy ensued, with orthodox bishops protesting this display of "syncretism" as antichristian and with much confusion among many other (less orthodox, but no less anxious) christians. How could a serious *christian* imply that a rain forest or a burning witch has a sacred spirit? Did she not know that there is only *one* true Spirit, only *one* God and Father of our Lord Jesus Christ? Is this where feminist liberation theology is leading?

Yes, feminist liberation theologies are leading us into spiritual communion with all creatures and, through them, close to the Holy One whom we meet in the struggles for justice that call us forth. Turning to the eagle, we see more clearly that God is indeed Many. The sacred Spirit soars through us as the movement for justice and compassion and meets us in many, infinitely many, "moments" in this movement through all time and eternity. She meets us in the sensuality of our embodied selves and as "other," stranger, alien. He howls in the coyote's call as surely as she chants the call to worship. She invites us to re-image *life*, whispering to us that life is more—and stranger—than it seems. God knows that life is more than a biological process that begins with a seed and a fertile womb. *Our life, our very soul*—as earth creatures together and individually—is a spirited process marked as much by disruption as by continuity and as much by brokenness and pain as by healing and happiness. Our life is a social and biological, political and emotional, historical and economic movement of energy and meaning and possibility. In the beginning and end of every "moment," *we* are a spiritual happening. And *our life* in the world of God is not centered around human beings any more than the cosmos is centered around the earth. The root of our salvation, call it christ/christa or God or love or justice, whatever names we may give it, does not have a single face. It has countless, different human faces and arms and amputations and also the faces and bodies of lambs and falcons and scorpions. Holy spirits? For sure! Many holy spirits to be respected and invoked and marveled at!

Ursula LeGuin writes:

By climbing up into his head and shutting out every voice but his own, "Civilized Man" has gone deaf. He can't hear the wolf calling him brother, not Master, but brother. He can't hear the earth calling him child—not Father, but son. He hears only his own words making up the world. He can't hear the animals. They have nothing to say. Children babble and have to be taught how to climb up into their heads and shut the doors of perception. No use teaching women at all, they talk all the time of course, but never say anything. This is the myth of Civilization, embodied in the monotheisms which assign soul to Man alone.[7]

So, are we christians being called to think again about monotheism—about what it actually may *mean* in, and for, our lives and for the life of the One who is Many? We dare not be smug about the turning, the conversion, required of us. Maybe we need to bow ourselves down before the bear and ask for forgiveness and help.

12

Sex and God
What Our Body Knows

In this essay, I want to look at what our bodies know and what, collectively, our body knows—we as church, we as society, we as human sisters and brothers.[1] What I mean is this: what our bodies and body can know insofar as we are honest with ourselves and one another about how we experience sex and how we experience God and what we think about sex and God.

Over the last fifteen years, I've discovered that coming out is an ongoing, surely a lifetime, process that has as much to do with spirituality as sexuality and everything to do with making and embodying connections between God and sex; between larger and smaller places of our love and work; between processes of healing and liberation; between experiences of sexual abuse and patriarchal christianity; between the well-being of our bodies and of this planet, our common body; among our racial, ethnic, class, sexual, and gender identities. Coming out is a matter of making connections with one another, spiritually as well as sexually. It is an ongoing process of revelation and manifestation, of incarnation and epiphany.

"Why do you tell us so much about yourself," some folks ask me. As a theologian, I offer images and stories and feelings much, I believe, as a gardener scatters seeds: in order to let them go and thereby to help them grow and multiply and feed those who come to a sacred harvest that is ours, not simply mine.

I have never regretted coming out. I love being lesbian! I delight in working theologically from the perspective of a woman whose embodied passion is generated primarily, not exclusively, in relation to her sisters here on the earth. And this, of course, has much to do with my experiences and understandings of our sacred power, the Spirit yearning for us, for life, for justice and joy and compassion.

A primary ethical problem facing the church in the realm of sex, gender, and power is *not* the lack of integrity in the personal relationships of lesbian, gay, bisexual, or heterosexual people. Rather, it is the *church's* lack of integrity as a historical, social institution, the church's ethic of sexual duplicity that requires good people to live lies. This is an ethical problem with which we gay and bisexual christians must wrestle. It is from this perspective on where the problem lies—with the church as an institutional body—that I speak.[2] The point should not be missed: *the church*—including all of us, regardless of our sexual identities—must carry the ethical burden together. It's not up to gay, lesbian, and bisexual members to carry this burden for the entire christian community. Indeed, we cannot.

Related to this is the church's belaboring of such issues as whether openly gay/lesbian folks can be ordained and whether the church should bless our relationships. Like the ordination of women and the ordination of Episcopalians of color, the answer to these questions is *simply yes, and now*. The most intriguing and significant conversations about sex and gender lie well beyond, though they are related to, such issues as ordained/sacramental ministry and relational blessing. I am referring to questions that will carry us well into the twenty-first century, questions such as whether gender—our maleness and femaleness—much less our sexual orientation or preference, is a fixed and static experience and conceptual category.

I believe the most pressing discourse on sexual morality, regardless of our sexual identity, is *not* about whether homosexuals "should" have sex but about what may constitute commitment, fidelity, and right, nonabusive relationship in our lives, whether we are gay, lesbian, bisexual, or heterosexual, and whether we are sexually active or celibate. How shall we, as christians, move the discourse on sexuality into the love, work, and sexuality of everyone? How shall we insist that we, especially the church, get honest?

How can we help one another do this? Can we help one another understand sexuality as a resource for making right relation and, conversely, right relation as a resource for expressing sexuality? Life in the world of God, after all, is not linear! And if sexuality can be a resource for right, mutually empowering, nonabusive relation, can it not be a sacred source, a text through which the Spirit moves us, a resource for goodness and godding?[3] Might our sexuality be both a root and flower of our life in the Spirit? These are some of the questions with which we as christians of different colors and cultures ought to be wrestling, learning from one another, allowing our differences in color, culture, sexuality, class, and gender to teach us all.

Come with me a little further into such theological musing, thinking about God and sex together. Can you imagine acceptance of the relationship of these two concepts? Can you imagine a high holy day in which sexuality is celebrated as sacrament? If you listen carefully to the backlash against feminist and womanist spiritualities and theologies these days, you'll notice that it is precisely this fear that is driving the campaigns against gays, lesbians, and feminists in the churches.[4] The fear is that if we *really* celebrate women, *really* celebrate sexuality, all of us (men, too) will wind up as lesbian pagans, worshiping the Wisdom/Sophia of God and emanating sensuality and passion from our bodies on the church's high holy days. God forbid!

Let's go a little further into what the religious right, and perhaps even much of the left (such as it is), so fears about the gay/lesbian agenda in the churches. I believe they (in all honesty, we, too) fear knowing consciously—intellectually, ethically, and responsibly—what our bodies know already and what our corporate body also knows, insofar as we allow ourselves to take seriously one another's feelings, fears, hopes, and yearnings for intimacy with one another and with God. We *know* we want and need and deeply desire connection—sturdy sensual bonding—with humans, with creatures, with and in sacred Spirit, a depth and quality of re- latedness that gives life and energy and desire for more con- nection. In essence, we yearn for genuinely *mutual* relation.

You may protest that many of us are so badly broken from abuse that we *cannot* yearn for mutuality, that we don't even know what it is; that we are too out of touch with our capaci- ties to harm others and/or to be harmed to risk such relation; that, as victims, we are too frightened to risk such desire; and that, as victims and/or perpetrators of abuse, our "bound- aries" are still too unformed for us to experience genuine mutuality. I hear such protesting a lot and I frankly hear it largely as a way of making excuses for not changing— excuses for not changing the systems of domination and con- trol, and excuses for not changing our lives as victims and/or as perpetrators of wrong relation.

Mutuality, like everything else, is learned by experiencing it, by trial and effort, by making mistakes and plodding on. This is how sex and God are "learned" as well—by risking intimacy, daring to let ourselves learn how to feel and listen to what our bodies and those of others can tell us about what we and others do (and do not) want, need, and desire.

Notwithstanding christian religious and modern secular

efforts to keep God and sex separate, the fact is our corporate body can know because, as bodies, we can know the Spirit incarnate, the sacred source of our hungry flesh, a deity not "above" or "beyond" the sensual, watery, bloody stuff that is us. In those moments when we really meet one another, our christic body knows what our bodies know: that God is with, and in, and through us, transcending our boundaries and particularities, connecting us with one another and, indeed, with those and that which *are* above and beyond us, in our past, in our future, in this world, and, from an ecological-theological perspective, in other worlds as well. Our bodies can and often do know.

We can know, through our bodies, that making sexual love to a *beloved* partner and worshiping the sacred Spirit of the worlds, Spirit of life, sacred source of history, alpha and omega of nature, are human experiences with much divinity in common. In our sexuality and our spirituality, we are vulnerable, opening to someone or something we *trust* to be there with us, wrestling with us, holding and comforting us, sharing pleasure and peace. We can know this—intellectually, theologically—because we can learn it from our bodies.

I am speaking of an epistemology of embodiment as the basis of both our understanding of ourselves as our church (who we are as a corporate body) and our theological anthropology (who we are in right relation to one another as sisters and brothers and friends and lovers). Whether in liturgy, in bed, or over a meal, we can know God and ourselves in relation to God through our feelings, the openings of our bodies, our swellings, wetness, heat, and cold, our hunger to take into ourselves the very essence of the beloved—literally, to eat and drink the one whom we love. Is this really so strange a notion for sacramental christians?

How much of our sex talk, what we say to our partner during sex, represents—in sex, through sex, with our partner

—a language also of spirituality, of deep yearning for security and assurance and joy and pleasure beyond what is either rational or controllable: a desire for God?

But who or what is this God? Can it be the Sacred One of Jews or of christians or must it be some other? Can our erotic power be the God whom Jesus loved? Or is such a spirit largely the reflection of that lustful desire which the christian mainline, since Augustine, has characterized as sin?

This is the theo-ethical juncture—between God and sex —at which feminists, womanists, and radical women theologians across cultures and religions, as well as gay men and lesbians, in my opinion, have the most *distinctive* contributions to make to religion and theology. Although what we teach about God and sex may not be, in every instance, the most pressing dimension of our work, to us or others, it is our *unique and special* offering to theological discourse. This is because we women and gay/lesbian people, be we white or black or yellow or brown, are (with a few exceptions such as Jim Nelson and Tom Driver) the *only* theologians of our century who seem to have noticed fundamental theological, ethical, and pastoral connections among what the church has taught about God, gender, and sexuality and to have noticed furthermore that these connections often constitute life-and-death issues for women, children, and marginalized men in all races and cultures, and thus are *not* merely the sex-fantasy-escape musings of white, socially privileged people.

From a liberation perspective, it cannot surprise us that those who notice a connection between God and sex are those who have been violated by it most consistently and reprehensibly. I mean by this women in patriarchal societies and especially women of color, poor women, and sexually deviant women like lesbians, single women, divorced women, and prostitutes; women in a racist, capitalist patriarchy that has been shaped culturally by christian teachings on God, gender, and sexuality *and* on race, religion, work, and economics.

What we have noticed, theologically, we women of different colors, gay men, lesbians, and other sexual deviants is that God and sex go hand in hand—or, more accurately in patriarchal religious cultures, penis in vagina. We have noticed that this patriarchal father/god is a deity of domination and entitlement, the projection of men who either assume they are or aspire to be lords and fathers of all, worshiped *because* they control. In this racist, sexist world, male sexuality —especially, though not exclusively, white male sexuality— is an instrument of control.

Let me say here, as clearly as I can, that I do *not* assume *all* white males experience their sexuality this way. I do assume that those males, white and other, who do not experience their sexuality this way have been shaped sexually by nondominant psychospiritual forces (men who genuinely are gentle, men who do not want badly to win, for example). I believe that such men are invariably exceptions to what is normative for "real men" in this predominantly christian, capitalist culture. I also believe that such men, of whatever color, religion, class, or sexuality, suffer a great deal because they are "not normal."

And because feminist, womanist, *mujerista,* and radical christian women see this and know it, through experience as well as education, it is theologically evident to us that this patriarchal god image does not accurately reflect *our* God, who is not a master of control, sexually or otherwise. An epistemology of embodiment keeps us theologically informed. We recognize false images of God, idols, pretense of love, because our bodies tell us what is what. Our bodies tell us that the power of love itself, the ongoing resource of encouragement and tenderness in our lives and the life of all creation, does not pry open the legs of little girls at night or get a hard-on while beating a woman or shove weapons of war up the anuses of vanquished soldiers. The God whom Jesus loved was, and is, no master of control.

Might God be, however, the master of men's *self*-control? From a feminist liberation perspective, this sounds promising. For how grand it would be, we imagine, if men—those who rule nations as well as families—were to control their sexual behavior—putting it bluntly, to keep their penises in their pants, as a bishop reportedly admonished the priests in his diocese.

But some feminist theologians also notice that such an ethic, and God, of self-control, has been the prevailing sexual ethic and theology for much of the church's history. We have lived with such an ethic for two thousand years. Given what we know today through psychology about repression, through biology and psychology about the force of sexual hunger, and through feminist theory about the tenacity of patriarchal power relations, we can perhaps imagine that a God of "self-control" may be, more truthfully, a deity constructed by men in order to be ignored by them. We should not be surprised that *despite* all the rules of celibacy, asceticism, and tight sexual control, bishops, priests, deacons, pastors, religious and lay people, men, women, and teenagers, of all colors and cultures and sexual identities, seem to heed their sexual appetites more than the doctrines and disciplines of the churches. If God *is* a master of self-control, christians on the whole have never had much of a relationship with Him, and we have no reason to imagine that this will change, even under the threat of litigation that is so popular today.

How much more responsible and creative, liberating and enduring, a spirituality if God were no master at all, no God of control, of self or others, but rather the eternal source of our capacities to love—to create right relation with one another, *not* by controlling ourselves or others but by being present with one another as sisters, brothers, and friends! The churches should be helping us cultivate this way of being together, in mutually empowering relational *struggle*—never perfect, never without mistakes, but bound together by a

commitment to learn together more fully how to be ourselves, in right relation.

Such a theology of mutual relation, of knowing and be
known, of struggling to know and be and do what we will
never "master," is a splendid task for us christians, a task to
be shared in a spirit of compassion and respect for differences. Theology is an ongoing process of critical reflection
together, as a body, on our relationships to that which we experience as sacred, source of creative and liberating power,
God. To imagine that we can find *the* theology or *the* ethics
that we need and that we can at that time stop thinking is like
assuming that because we've tasted an excellent meal, we
must eat only the same meal again and again if we are to be
well fed. We are not through thinking about sex and gender
and power and God. We are not through theologically or
ethically, pastorally or biblically, biologically or sociologi-
cally, anthropologically or historically. We will never be
through!

Can this promise elicit our gratitude and acceptance or will
we resist believing what our bodies know: that whatever is
not changing and growing is dead?

13

Body of Christa
Hope of the World

You have asked me to discuss hope. I am glad to think with you about the hope that does not disregard the violence, poverty, terror, and confusion in our lives and those of other sisters and brothers. Any "hope" that tries not to see the massive suffering of the world, as evidenced by the street children here in Salvador (Bahia, Brazil) and teenage prostitutes in Manila and Los Angeles, is not hope at all. To the contrary, it reflects a sense of powerlessness and an abdication of responsibility that too often passes for "spirituality."

We must say no to this spirituality of despair, recognizing that, in our churches today, in the North and the South, the West and the East, it is a serious theological problem. This cynical spirituality is an ethical and pastoral problem cultivated through the highly individualistic economy and social relations of global capitalism. We christians need to help one another understand that the economic and spiritual supports of any culture always lean heavily on each other and that throughout the world, among richer and poorer peoples, an individualistic global economic movement and many privatistic pieties being spawned by it are holding our societies and our souls hostage.

With sisters and brothers of other faiths, we christians need liberation. With our *compañeras* of other religious traditions, we also are being called in this *kairos*, this sacred moment, to embody good news of liberation to the oppressed. We are called to bear together a power that is the hope of the world. We are called to participate with ever-greater clarity and courage in God's ongoing work of redemption.

Before I go further, I want to name my anger as a white, middle-strata, Episcopalian, a United States citizen with English roots who shares the guilt and privileges of my people. The people of the United States on the whole are not a joyful people. We are not spiritually at peace. We are a troubled, turbulent people, breeding addiction, abuse, and poverty among ourselves. Capitalism has not satisfied our deeply human yearning to be in right relation with our sisters and brothers and it never will. This is because advanced patriarchal capitalism is a political, economic, and spiritual movement founded upon the sanctity of the freedom of ruling-class males to do as they please—to own, control, and increase their property, including women, children, men whom they have made their slaves, and other creatures who serve as their subordinates. So there is little real joy these days in the United States and a great deal of suffering and shame. I believe that the most joyful people are those actively involved in the struggles for justice and compassion and that, therefore, in the struggle is our happiness.

Many of us realize that what may appear to be grand and inviting in tourist brochures for New York, Rio, London, Capetown, Tokyo, or Sydney reflects, in fact, a global context of economic triage. In this system of selective death, increasing numbers of women, children, and men (especially, but not only, in the southern hemisphere) and increasing amounts of natural resources such as rain forests, rivers, and farmlands are being eliminated so that 1 or 2 percent of the people on the earth can continue to expand their wealth. This is happening both globally and locally. The richer northern nations are exploiting the economically dependent southern nations, and within the nations themselves—such as the United States, Brazil, South Africa, Korea—richer people are getting richer and poorer people are getting poorer, one day at a time, every day. These national situations increasingly are bound up in advanced patriarchal capitalism's global movement.

So what is the church to do in the midst of what UNICEF (the United Nations children's organization) has called "an outrage against a large section of humanity," referring to the more than 500,000 children in the world who, in 1988 alone, died in the two-thirds world as a direct result of the International Monetary Fund's "structural adjustment programs"? These SAP's are global capitalism's primary means of "adjusting" economic conditions and organizing indigenous peoples—often women's labor in the two-thirds world—so as to maximize the profit for the rich in both north and south. We no longer have to come to Washington, Miami, Boston, or Los Angeles to find the so-called "ugly American"—the rich white man who exploits the poor of Latin America, Africa, or Asia. We find his clone today throughout the world.

I want to offer an image of what we christians can do and be in this world. I am thinking of Edwina Sandys's sculpture *Christa*. I believe we are called today to love, honor, and liberate *el cuerpo de la Crista*, the Body of Christa.

We see her before us, hanging on the cross, in her many contemporary forms, the body of bleeding, broken women:
• We remember slave women—servant women: Christa.
• We remember battered and sexually abused women: Christa.
• We remember women gone mad as the only way to survive violence: Christa.
• We remember 200,000 Korean women servicing Japanese soldiers: Christa.

- We remember hundreds of thousands of Filipina women used by U.S. soldiers: Christa.
- We remember countless African American women abused by white men, often with the complicity of white women: Christa.
- We remember the increasing numbers of Latin American women being used by multinational corporations to advance the profit from the south: Christa.
- We remember teenage girls raped by those whom they trust and children forced to bear unwanted children: Christa.
- We remember Palestinian women and children, Iraqi women, Serbian, Croatian, and Bosnian women, Tibetan women, women of East Timor, of Ethiopia, Somalia, Zaire, Kenya, South Africa—women and children burned, raped, hungry; starving women, children, and powerless men around the world—*el cuerpo de la Crista*.

Some time ago, when the Christa sculpture was put on display in New York's Episcopal Cathedral of St. John the Divine, her presence generated such a stir that the bishop had her taken down. It seemed that, for many people, the image of a naked, crucified woman was neither sacred nor bearable. Like all women experienced as confrontative or challenging to patriarchal power, the Christa sculpture is controversial. Lots of folks don't like her. Like Christa, and with her, we cannot expect simultaneously to help make God incarnate in the world and be affirmed by those holding patriarchal power in place.

But we can help one another take being controversial in stride. For whoever led us to imagine that we can follow Jesus, our brother and liberator, and expect to be affirmed by those who hold institutional power in place? What fluff-brained thinking has led us to imagine that we can open our minds and lives to the God whom Jesus loved and expect to be admired by everyone?

Until ten other women deacons and I were ordained to the

priesthood "irregularly" in 1974, we had been experienced, I suppose, as "nice" women. But this changed the moment we stood up for women—ourselves and others. A sister priest sent me a postcard the other day with these words by Rebecca West on it: "I myself have never known what feminism is. I only know that people call me a feminist whenever I express sentiments that differentiate me from a doormat." I suggest that women must give up our efforts to be nice and our willingness to be doormats. Don't mistake me: We can be caring and at times gentle, but if we are committed to the work of justice making with compassion and peace, we will not be nice women.

But I am writing here of *hope*! In what sense is Christa's body our hope? Hope is not a static quality or state of being. Like faith and love, hope is a way of being, a relational dynamic. In speaking of Christa as our hope, I want to suggest three particularly "Anglican" ways of understanding this hope—through sacrament, participation, and reformation.

SACRAMENT

We are a *sacramental* church, in which we share the *real presence* of God. If we seriously believe in God's incarnate presence with us, then we share God by being really present with one another. This is the foundation of our Catholic legacy. Bishop Ed Browning has spoken of this: not simply that we have "sacraments" in the church but that what we share in liturgy is a way of imaging, remembering, and celebrating what we share in life, wherever we are and with whomever. I agree with Ed Browning. A sacramental way of seeing and living requires that we look at what is really happening, that we face the truth, that we see ourselves as we are in relation to one another, that we be really present with one another.

What does it mean for us to face the body of Christa in this way? To be really present with her? Does it not mean we must look honestly at the pain of our sisters, those whom we know well, those whom we do not know as well, and—when it is in our own personal pain—that we must look as truthfully as we can at our own lives and try to see what is going on?

Christa is an appropriate image for that which is sacred in our midst. Recognizing her reality, whatever we may call her, is basic to our ability to live in spiritual continuity with Jesus. For the memory and presence of Jesus with us today draws us to the margins, the poor, the outcast, and despised —Christa, *el cuerpo de la Crista*.

And who are these poor women? If we are indigenous women in the Americas, they are our mothers and grand-mothers, passing on their oral traditions, their survival stories, their sacred stories, for seven generations.

Who are these outcasts? If we are Hispanic or African American women in New York City, they are our children killing one another with drugs sold and guns bought in order to survive the racism and poverty of our culture of despair.

Who are these despised? They are women, children, and marginalized men held in contempt because they are experi-enced by those with social and economic power as "prob-lems" that can't be solved, "embarrassments" that can't be faced, forces "out of control"—like women seeking repro-ductive freedom; women struggling against sexual violence in our homes, churches, and communities; women acting sexually with men or women *as we please*.

Women poor, women outcast, women despised—*el cuerpo de la Crista*.

Can you think of a more authentic image for our time than that of the young Korean woman whose body was used sixty times a day by Japanese soldiers and who went mad?[1] Surely, *the Body of Christa*.

Or of the African woman brought in chains to the United States, often to be raped, always to be owned by white men. She who was beaten, her children abused, her children sold.

She who still today is violated, disregarded, her children taken from her in a culture of racist poverty, genocide, and despair? *The Body of Christa* indeed.

Our call from God is to stand with Christa, lend her our voice, pledge her our commitment, be present with her. When we face her, we recognize ourselves as we truly are connected with one another, sisters and brothers in the world. When we are honest about our connectedness and the responsibility we bear with and for one another, our lives become more fully linked materially and spiritually. We actually share a common body—Christa—amidst our differences of color, class, culture, religion, sexual identity, age, and ability. Meeting together as sisters, we are a stronger body, Christa. And if we choose to stand together, we pay the price. For we cannot avoid suffering with those with whom we truly stand. I think, for example, of Maria Cueto of Los Angeles and Raisa Nemikin, her *compañera*, two brave women employees from the Episcopal Church, U.S.A., who in the 1970s refused to cooperate with the FBI in its harassment of Puerto Rican independence activists in the United States.

In joining our lives and work with those who suffer oppression, we become the body of Christa, a sacrament to be shared on behalf of life fully lived. Anglicanism is a sacramental tradition. We are called to be faithful to this tradition —to be really present, to make ourselves known, to be *a living sacrament*, which is a much better image than "living sacrifice," because it is life-affirming and holistic and signals more fully a celebration of ourselves in right relation.

How can we Anglicans live more sacramentally as a church? How can we be clear that "sacrament" is only secondarily about what we receive on Sunday morning at church? How can we, among the richer and poorer in the South and the North, help one another realize that to be a sacramental people is to be a people really present with

Christa, loving her body? Standing with the poor, the suffering, the marginalized of our cities, countryside, and churches and, in so doing, making Christa more fully visible in and to the world? How can we be one Body, with her? One Body of Christa, ourselves both victim and redeemer, She who is crucified, She who is rising?

The way the institutional church could be one with Christa would be to risk losing whatever social, economic, or political security we may have. I mean that if we are seriously interested in Christa, we christians in the United States cannot continue to cooperate with the state's economic policies that benefit the rich at the expense of the poor. We christians cannot continue to support racist policies that benefit people with roots in northern Europe at the expense of people from Asian, African, and Latin cultures. As christians, we cannot lend our support to policies designed to promote an accumulation of profit at the expense of the earth's survival. And, if we are committed to Christa, we who are christian women cannot uphold heterosexist policies that perpetuate patriarchal values, whatever their cultural roots, at the expense of most women and children and also of lesbians and gay men, who embody a special challenge to the traditional "rights" of kings and fathers to possess, name, and control the world and who, therefore, are especially feared and despised.

One of the few times in recent memory I have been proud to be an Episcopalian was when Bishop Browning met with the president of the United States to speak out against the war in the Persian Gulf. This was a wonderfully public display of peace making, justice seeking, and christic presence confronting institutional power. Like Bishop Browning, the rest of us also are called to speak out and act up on behalf of justice in the world and church. Such courage and leadership should be the rule of christian life, not an exception. We ought not to be surprised when a christian leader does something publicly on behalf of justice.

PARTICIPATION

We Anglicans also have an understanding of "participation" that is fundamental to our tradition, a doctrine articulated in the work of Richard Hooker, sixteenth-century English theologian. There is a strong spiritual link between our *mutuality* (we all have much to give and receive from one another) and *participation* (by our birthrights we are members of the same Body, called to share in the ongoing creation and suffering, liberation and blessing of the world). Someone who has touched me in my spiritual pilgrimage has been the Vietnamese Buddhist Thich Nhat Hahn, poet and peace activist. "Please call me by my true name so I can wake up," he writes. "So the door to my heart can be opened: the door of compassion."[2] Immersed in life, we are people of passion, living fully, suffering deeply. We know one another and we know one another's passion. We literally suffer injustice, pain, and grief with one another—just as we celebrate life and joy, justice and peace with one another. Being with one another in joy and in sorrow, in celebration and in pain, generates our *compassion*, our passion-with-one-another.

Compassion is the lens through which we see that we are connected to everyone and everything that has gone before us, that which is with us now on the earth, and that which will come after us. *Compassion is a deep knowledge of the heart that our lives and labors are joined at the root. It enables us to struggle passionately against injustice without forgetting that our enemies are still our brothers and sisters.* We may, and often do, set ourselves against our enemies, but we accord them the respect that every creature deserves, however reprehensible his or her behavior. There is no more sacred quality than compassion: to look upon our enemies, those who might wish us harm, with a respect steeped in a realization that those who would harm us do not know what they are doing. They may know it rationally, but they do not know it spiritually. For in bringing harm, suffering, or death to their brothers and sisters, they are out of touch with the Spirit of God and, as such, are meandering about in that place of loneliness and torture that is "hell."

Compassion reminds us that we ourselves walk close to hell and sometimes in it and that it is by the grace and power of God mediated to us most often by these who do not forget us, but continue to reach out for us, that we are, in any given historical moment, people of joy and compassion rather than people of loneliness and despair, contempt and fear. When we are ourselves as we are meant to be—ourselves in right relation, "called by our true name"—we are people of compassion which enables us to develop an ethic of nonviolence, forgiveness, and humility. This should be the essence of christian faith, my friends—not an option, but the very core of who we are, mutual participants in life.

What this may mean for Anglicans is likely to be unsettling, because we are called by the sacred Spirit to be sisters, brothers, and friends in the world. We are *not* called to be bishops, priests, deacons, and lay people. We are not ordered hierarchically by the Spirit. This is something we have done to ourselves in spite of other spiritual possibilities. I believe that, in the coming century, if we as a species are still alive, we christians must be on our way toward becoming non-hierarchical, sacramental communities of faith and cross-cultural perspectives. We Anglicans should be strengthening our sacramental and participatory character which, I believe, someday will involve giving up our "orders" of ministry.

Resources from which we could draw in this work might include various indigenous and other non-European perspectives on sacred power, women's spirituality, and our historical Jewish religious roots. Of course, to draw upon resources from the traditions of those whom we christians have violated—such as indigenous peoples, Africans, Asians, women, gay and lesbian people, Jews, Muslims, and many others—requires humility, repentance, and commitment to mutuality. Only in such a spirit might we proceed toward becoming liberating churches of genuinely sacramental presence and mutual participation, not only among ourselves as christians but also with others.

REFORMATION

We can change because we are a *reformation* church. We are catholic sacramentalists and participants, but we are also protestant. This third characteristic—having roots in protest, dissent, and change—can give us hope in these times, for it suggests that neither we nor the world is finished. The revolution is never won.

Throughout my brief time in Brazil, the strongest sentiment women voiced to me was that the Anglican church and its "Decade on Evangelism" has completely disregarded women's well-being and women's concerns. There is much anger about this. I hope we will take this anger back to our nations and churches and be angry, caring agents of reform. After all, if we are not participants in reformation, why are we here? And if we are, we cannot return home without renewed resolve to make no peace with oppression and violation of women in our cultures, countries, and churches.

I have a story that may illustrate how reformation can take root. It's a story about some white, suburban, Episcopal women in the United States. I dedicate it to every woman who's ever been told that the reason something can't be done—like ordaining women or permitting reproductive freedom—is because women either don't want it or can't handle it.

A number of years ago, I was invited to speak on "spirituality" to an Episcopal group of about twenty-five women. I was surprised because Episcopalians who don't know me well seldom associate me with "spirituality." I spent quite a bit of time thinking and praying about this particular meeting. As it happened, I was arrested in a demonstration against the Nicaraguan *contra* on the morning of the evening on which my presentation was to be given and I wound up in jail. It wasn't clear I'd be released in time for the evening meeting, but, in the meantime, I had the entire day to think about what I might say if I were able to attend.

I did get to the meeting and spoke briefly about five experiences in my adult life in which I'd had a strong sense of the presence of God: (1) working with Nicaraguans, Salvadoreans, U.S. citizens, and others for justice and peace in Central America; (2) my father's death and my family's grief; (3) having a lump removed from my breast which moved me to a new level of awareness of my body, "womanness," and finitude; (4) being ordained a priest in the "irregular" service in 1974; and (5) five years later, my decision to come out as a lesbian woman, priest, and theologian. I spoke of why each of these contexts seemed to me a fertile ground for spiritual movement and of what I had learned about God through these experiences.

Soon into the evening other women began to speak of their lives in relation to the Spirit. They shared stories and images of their bodies, children, families, work, love, and aspirations. They spoke of fear and despair, of courage and hope. They talked about having gay kids and the force of homophobia in their children's lives. They discussed the United States and how powerless they often feel in the face of massive wrongs perpetuated by our government. They related anxieties about their bodies, mastectomies, eating disorders, and lack of self-esteem. They spoke about the men in their lives, about the church, about violence against women, about sexuality and desire.

As the evening progressed, the women reflected on sources of empowerment, courage, and hope in their lives. They named prayer, study, art and drama, consciousness raising, anger at injustice, mentors and teachers, community organizing on small and larger scales, and the power of friendship as important spiritual resources. I imagine that most, probably all, of the women present were touched and changed that night, empowered in small ways to live with greater self-confidence and a stronger commitment to justice.

This occasion was filled with the Spirit. Together, we *were* the body of Christa that evening—Christa in us, we in Christa—sisters, all of us changers, all of us changing, through our mutual participation in a process of healing and liberation in which each woman's pain became a little more bearable because it was shared. As it happened, we did not celebrate a eucharist on that occasion, but we most assuredly made a holy communion together for we were fed and empowered by the Spirit.

The Anglican traditions of sacrament, participation, and reform give us a sturdy historical foundation on which to build our church as women really present with one another and with the men in our lives; women committed to facing, naming, and sharing life as we actually experience it, allowing our christian theologies to blossom, fresh, sweet, and tenacious because they are real.

14

Re-Imagining
A Conversation—Carter Heyward and Beverly Harrison

One of the most emphatic recent portends of the hard times faced by feminists struggling to be faithful to the liberation tradition within christianity has been the violent and virulent reaction within the churches to "Re-Imagining: A Global Theological Conference by Women for Women and Men," held in Minneapolis in November 1993. It was attended by "some 2,200 women and 83 brave men from many denominations" and guided by thirty prominent women theologians who served as major speakers and workshop leaders.[1] Those who attended the conference praised it as one of the most multi-cultural, creative, spirited events they had ever experienced.

Several protestant denominations—especially the United Presbyterian and United Methodist churches, both of which had large numbers of participants—have experienced fierce denunciation of the event and efforts to punish any who identify publicly with the conference. Church members have withheld money, demanded (successfully in the case of a courageous Presbyterian, Mary Ann Lundy) that women who helped fund, plan, or lead the conference be fired, and insisted that the denominations repudiate the conference and everything it stood for. Of special concern seems to have been the worship of Sophia (replacing Jesus, critics charge), the liturgical sharing of milk and honey (instead of bread and wine), and the moment in the conference when about a hundred lesbian participants responded to an invitation from United Church of Christ minister Melanie Morrison to affirm their lesbianism publicly as a source of special power.[2] Some Presbyterian and Methodist leaders insist that Re-Imagining has sparked the most serious crisis in the churches in decades, and many women who attended are under siege. Progressive christians realize increasingly that the reaction against the Re-Imagining conference was organized by the Political Right using the churches to further its own agenda. Still, many of us agree that the conference and the reaction against it signal a theological watershed for twentieth-century christianity. With this in mind, I asked Beverly Harrison, ever a beloved friend and companion, to join me in a conversation about the significance of this event, which she attended and I did not.

CH: I'll start off by noting something we've already discussed, along with Barbara Lundblad, Kwok Pui-lan, Delores Williams, and others: The reaction to the conference has been so racist. The conference, I've heard from you and others, was wonderfully multi-cultural. The responses of these mainline churches reminds me of the orthodox reaction to Chung Hyun Kyung's presentation in Canberra in 1991. These churches condemn what spirited women are doing without recognizing not only the misogyny, sexism, homophobia, and heterosexism but also the racism and cultural imperialism in their responses.

BH: I agree, but the problem is that the eurocentric white churches do not understand their own racism. They see no connection between their theological stance, their notion of one unequivocal truth which *they* possess and which they require everyone else to consent to, as racist. But, of course, this absolutist theological stance is the heart of racism as it is also the core of sexism. The actual historical patterns of injustice are always entangled whether white people see it or not. Look at *The Presbyterian Layman*, for example. When it began battering the conference and chose to manipulate and distort the meaning of Delores Williams's serious, substantive questions about the doctrine of the atonement, I'm not sure these right-wing people who inveighed against her lecture were even aware that she is an African American. But the criticism is still racist, because it presumes one, single, uniform theological truth that everyone of any racial/ethnic community and culture has to conform to—and that truth, of course, was defined in Europe as "Christianity." It's going to take a lot of work to get white christians to understand this because, right now, the churches' reactions are so fear-based that they cannot hear what we're saying. To the charge that their responses to Re-Imagining were both racist and sexist, they just say, "No, that's a ridiculous accusation."

CH: One thing we women need to make increasingly central to our theological work is that race and culture have to be held together. You're right that most people would deny that their responses to Delores, or Pui-lan, or Hyun Kyung were racist, because a lot of people do not see that what is being called for is that eurocentric culture, including european christianity, reign supreme *theologically* as it does throughout western societies, and this culture has largely been defined and shaped by white males. The theological doctrine of the atonement is a cultural construct that had benefitted white christian men in particular ways—it's enabled them, for example, not to feel as guilty for their *countless* crucifixions of the world's poor, people of color, women, Jews, people of other religious and ethnic traditions, animals, and the earth. There are two primary problems with these classical atonement traditions: one is that they suggest, erroneously, that Jesus' suffering was "good"—good for God and good for humans—and therefore that in order for us to be "good" we have to suffer, too. When preached by priests and other ecclesiastical authorities to others—often to women and others marginalized in church and society—this message is sadistic and perverse. The other atonement teaching that is seriously flawed from a feminist and womanist perspective is that since, through Christ's death and resurrection, the victory of life over death is already won, we don't need to worry much about the state of the world. It's already "saved." Ethically, this is a pernicious assumption that undercuts the commitment to seek justice and love mercy, and it certainly moves against the well-being of most humans and creation. But how many white male theologians, even among our best friends and allies, do you think understand the racism in traditional christian theologies?

BH: Most white people think of racism merely as having negative feelings about other people, which they can deny they have. The *essence* of racism is cultural imperialism and the eurocentric monopoly epistemology: "There is one objective truth and we possess it"—this is its essence. The rest of the world must be dictated to accordingly. It's the point you and I have made many times: the difference is between the spirituality underlying capitalism and the spirituality underlying native peoples. It is the capitalist assumption that there is a limited supply of Truth, possessed by particular people, versus an understanding of truth as abundantly springing from different peoples' experiences. The West is in crisis. We are destroying Mother Earth, raping the earth and our own communities, making them fear-based, demanding that people conform to things that aren't good for them, doing this all to ourselves as well. I believe this spirituality of monopoly capitalism is running rampant around the world, seeking to kill those who don't conform, those who have another epistemology, a vision of abundant life and abundant truth—the vision that was celebrated in the Re-Imagining conference!

CH: Yes, and that's why the conference has been called a theological watershed. I think that is true—and that, in order to understand it, the conference has to be seen in the context of the feminist, womanist, *mujerista,* and various liberation theologies of the last several decades. Many strong liberation currents flow into the watershed, making it what it is—a signal that the spirituality of racist patriarchal capitalism is in serious trouble. Two years ago Chung Hyun Kyung and I were speakers at the Anglican Women's Encounter in Brazil. She spoke primarily on sexuality and I focused on the ravages of capitalism.[3] Some of the conference planners resisted including our contributions in reports on the event because "not all the planners agreed with us."

BH (laughing): If only we could suppress the opinion of every male theologian not everyone agrees with!

CH: Indeed! I guess "agree" is the wrong word here. The women who *affirmed* what Hyun Kyung and I were trying to do were many of the Anglican women from the "two-thirds" world—from Latin American, African, and Asian cultures—and the feminists and womanists from North America, Europe, Australia, and New Zealand. These women didn't care whether all or, for that matter, any of the women present "liked" what we said or agreed with us. They were just glad someone was saying what needed to be said about women's sexualities and about what the global economy is doing to women and children in particular.

BH: You're so right that this theological "re-imagining" has been in process among women of many racial/ethnic communities for a long time now. When the vicious attacks began on the Re-Imagining conference, as hateful and sick as they've been, I realized that we had been doing something *right*! That was the only way to explain this high-priced, media-orchestrated, violent assault on the conference. Somebody was really running scared. And I think it's because the conference was so amiable, not because it was so radical. The spirit was good, people named their issues, and there was some confrontation within an atmosphere of fundamental respect. I'm sure there were a few women there who found this to be pretty scary, because it wasn't the same old spiritual blathering they were used to, but most of the women understood that this was wonderfully creative spirituality, exciting and refreshing and good.

CH: Yes, *Sophia* was alive and active in the conference and connecting many women more deeply with the Jesus tradition in liberating ways. What these terrified christian leaders don't seem to get is that feminist spirituality can *transform* rather than eliminate christian faith. Or maybe they *do* get it, and the thought is threatening. Certainly, Sophia, as one of the *most* christian god-images, with deep Jewish roots, is likely to be a major source of theological "re-imagining" for many christian women. She certainly has been for me.

BH: That's true, but I'm concerned not only with christian women's spirituality but with the vast, global shift taking place. Increasing numbers of people are simply fed up with expressions of religion that are major forms of alienation. I mean, religion that is fear-based and controlling and arrogant. I wish I had a nickel for everyone who's said to me over the last few years, "I'm interested in spirituality, but not in religion." And I think the leadership of the churches knows that the tide has turned against them and they're blaming us for the product of their own fear-based rigidities. I think we're up against a very powerful crisis, a schism, a turning, in which the fear-based religious sensibilities that are always closely tied to white men's desire for control—we'll decide, we'll let you know what you should believe, we'll tell you what to do—are being left behind. Partly cause their worldview is so boring.

CH: But it's also dangerous because it provides the spiritual foundation for the right-wing political agenda.

BH: It always does. At the conference I called this anti-feminist, right-wing junk "Jurassic Park theology," because it is a contrived theological environment that reflects the fear-based illusions of white men about what the world and christianity was like when their grandfathers inhabited it. Such a world of "true faith" never existed, of course, but these men have to believe it did—and that is the basis of their christian ideology. They have to create the impression that there's a "safe place" where questions don't exist and differences have no place.

CH: And the Re-Imagining conference embodied something totally different, a way of being christian grounded in differences, mutuality, and a shared desire to be open to life as we and others actually live it. The conference was fully alive, while the public spiritualities of the mainline churches are dead and dying.

BH: Yes. What was so exciting, so refreshing and, from the Jurassic Park perspective, so new, was that *women* came together and embodied theologies and liturgies that were so very *excellent*. It laid to rest the distortion that only white ruling-class men can speak the truth of christianity for women, a distortion that historically has been the source of

disempowerment for women. At the Re-Imagining conference, women came together and saw through this lie. We experienced our own collective power to speak the truths of our
lives, learn from the differences among us, and re-envision
our traditions. But the male leadership of the churches will
go to any length to combat, distort, manipulate, and even kill
us if they must, in order not to be changed by us.

CH: We can be sure about that. I draw some lessons from the
struggle for women's ordination and, especially, the Episcopal church's response twenty years ago to our "irregular"
ordination.[4] There are several parallels, I believe, between
Re-Imagining and that earlier event: one is the fear-based,
mean-spirited reaction of church leaders. Another is that we
women need one another's solidarity in order to survive the
hate. And another is that the ordination, like Re-Imagining,
signaled a commitment from which there is no turning back:
feminist, womanist, and *mujerista* theologies are here to stay,
like women priests. On a more personal note, because we
women priests revealed ourselves in 1974 as so outrageous
and heretical, most of my theological work, as well as the
ministries of my "irregular" sisters, over the last two decades
has been either ignored entirely or distorted by those Episcopal church leaders and theologians who are terrified of feminism and, in my case, lesbianism as well. Of course, these
men (and a few women, too) have good reason to be scared
of us, because our ordination was truly a sign that things are
changing, and my "irregular" sisters and I on the whole have
continued to work for the theological and ecclesiastical transformation that our ordinations signaled. By Jurassic Park
standards, we were and are *bad* girls!

Women condemned in the aftermath of Re-Imagining
need to be aware that this kind of distortion and dismissal of
their work will continue to take place and to allow their support networks to help them take this professional violation in

stride. Everything *does* change following this kind of thing. Despite the cruelty and stupidity, much of what happens is very good!

I'm not sure any of the "irregular" priests would have survived had we not supported one another in whatever ways we could in the aftermath of the ordination. Our solidarity was our salvation at the time, and I don't mean by this close personal friendship or frequent communication but simply knowing that there were others in this situation with us, that we were sisters, and that we would not allow ourselves to be divided—in our case—into "bad" and "badder" girls on the basis of others' perceptions of who we were and are.

BH: I think that's exactly right. If you take any initiative as a woman, rather than following the expectations of those who see themselves in charge, *you* will be seen as violating others. I've heard you discuss the distortions of your theological work, and of your whole person, recently—and not just in the context of your ordination and its similarities to the Re-Imagining conference but also in relation to many women's rage against your most recent book.[5] I've heard you say on a number of occasions, and I agree with you entirely, that no one can raise fundamental questions about an institution and expect its leaders to be grateful. You are right: there's a lesson in this for participants in the Re-Imagining conference—we should expect violent responses. I mean, church leaders, like so many men, are in a frenzy about women becoming empowered to live our own lives! Just look at what's getting played out on television right now in the wake of the arrest of O. J. Simpson for the murders of Nicole Brown Simpson and Ronald Goldman. Everywhere we turn, more violence against women.

CH: Let's talk for a minute about the reaction to the coming out of lesbians at the conference. Maybe one hundred or so out of more than two thousand women came out at Melanie Morrison's invitation. I wonder how close this was to the core of the church's agitation about this conference. My experience as a lesbian is that we who are "out" represent an embodiment of erotic power and passion—whether or not we individually feel this or think of ourselves this way—and that the christian churches really cannot tolerate large numbers of "out" lesbians because we represent much of what christian tradition has condemned as sinful or dangerous—being women for starters, having sex for pleasure (and with women), taking women's bodies seriously, not being "obedient" to male partners, being living embodiments of a wholesale defiance of christian teachings on sex and women. How basic do you think this has been to the churches' reaction to the conference?

BH: As I said before, I think this "crisis"—the churches' ugly reaction—is entirely orchestrated. Let's be very clear about this. The first public news accounts I saw came from letters to the editors in Minneapolis newspapers. These were libelous diatribes written by people who hadn't been at the conference. Much of this—a pasting together of various distortions of what had been said and done—is still assumed to be true. Except for accounts written by those in attendance, nothing I've read had anything to do with what really had happened. After the churches began to beat up on some of the women who were there and to try to find out from them something about what this "terrible conference" had been about, no doubt a few recanted and admitted they were shocked at some things that had occurred. We know there are always lesbians to be blamed whenever women are perceived as out of control! So maybe there was a delayed reaction of homophobia by some women attendees. But mostly I think what occurred was that some male thugs have decided to use Re-Imagining as a means of regaining control of the church

and to try to discredit the rising tide of women who are beginning to wear feminist and womanist and *mujerista* lenses in
formulating their faith.

What actually happened at the conference itself was that
lesbians were invited to step forward as a group and come
out because so little attention had been paid earlier in the
conference to lesbianism as a theological issue. It had been
planned that someone would address the issue later in the
conference, probably because the planners were a little timid.
But, in any case, when Melanie Morrison invited lesbians to
stand and come forth to form a circle, about one hundred of
us did, including some women who had never been public
before about being lesbians. The entire conference was at that
point deeply moved, because this group of lesbians included
a number of women deeply beloved by many there. Many
delegates were weeping openly, not only out of admiration
and appreciation for the courage being demonstrated, but
also because all were aware of the cost of being lesbian in our
homophobic churches. The women at the conference had an
opportunity, for just a moment, to bear witness and pay trib-
ute to many dearly beloved and respected lesbians sisters who
often are objects of such deep contempt in church circles.

And another thing was that everybody knew that because
of the depth of heterosexism in the church, there were many
wonderful women there who could *not* come forth, because
if they did they'd lose their jobs and be persecuted. At that
moment, some of these women were feeling awful. What
happened at the conference was overwhelmingly wonderful!
However, beyond the conference, right-wing christians,
masters of *using* homophobia and heterosexism to exploit the
fears of church people, saw this opportunity. They bash gay
men and lesbians all the time and here was yet another way to
discredit the conference.

I also want to go back to our first point, racism, and say
that just as heterosexism really wasn't adequately addressed

in the conference, the same was true of white racism as a specific historical form of racism. This troubled not only the African American women and other non-European women who were there but others of us, too. There were not enough women of color present to get the issue raised, however, especially in a context in which, more broadly, racism as cultural imperialism was being taken very seriously. So, both heterosexism and white racism caused some tensions at the conference, but I really don't think many, if any, of the participants were initially upset that lesbians came out. They might have been a little shocked, because it was dramatic and such a very moving moment. But upset? No. I think the homophobia has been stirred up intentionally by the reactionaries as a way of galvanizing support for their fear-based agenda.

CH: Yes, I've heard from other sisters that two weaknesses in a fabulous conference were the invisibility of white-over-black racism and the tiptoeing around the theological significance of lesbianism, even though lesbians were wonderfully represented by sisters like Virginia Mollenkott and Mary Hunt and you, who work explicitly as lesbians. But perfection can't be our goal! And it must surely have been a remarkable, spirited conference.

BH: Yes, and I think it needs to be said here, and I've heard you say it many times, that some women have the luxury to come out and many others do not. It was mostly *white* women who came forward. There were lesbians of color there, but many of them do not have the luxury of coming out.

CH: Yes, it *is* a luxury; even among white women, it's a luxury that has to do with class and professional security and relational safety and all sorts of things. I've never doubted that my being white and relatively secure professionally in this society enabled me to come out when and as I did. I believe as much now as ever that we have to respect one another's ability or lack of ability to be out as lesbians and the choices we make about this. We have to be in solidarity with one another, in and out—that's imperative and a challenge. I also think it's just *wonderful* when lesbians can and do come out, and I want to encourage it. When that happens, ecclesiastical authorities usually freak-out because we're seen to embody and represent the demise of the church—which we do, of course, insofar as church, as you say, has become "Jurassic Park."

BH: The church is *so* ignorant about sexuality. Basically, the church teaches us that the world is flat when it comes to sexuality. These church leaders are so ignorant and so arrogant. They simply demand that christians believe that, when it comes to sexuality, there is one "normal," God-given reality. The world *is* flat and that's that! This is what's going to make this kind of white male theology increasingly a laughingstock among people who are tuned in to the real world and social, cultural, and scientific learning of the modern period.

CH: In the meantime, a lot of people will be bashed, of course, as these closed-minded christians and their counterparts in Islam and Judaism and other patriarchal religions around the world continue to insist that the world of eroticism must be experienced on their terms.

BH: We need to say this, and say it loud: closed-minded christians today are as blind to complex scientific learnings as the detractors of Copernicus and Galileo once were.

CH: In this context, what can we say to our sisters about survival and courage and strategy? How, for example, do teachers like us even begin to frame the task we share with our students as we try to cope with ethics and theology in this context?

BH: Well, when we feel overwhelmed because the men with wealth and control throughout the world are so violent with their "power of expertise," as well as the many other ways they violate women and marginalized men, we need to remember that we're the ones with the life! The passion! The creativity! That the power of God really is moving among us! We have to remember that we have a *right* to participate in the abundance of creation! We have a right to struggle toward abundant life! Our womanist sisters have taught us that faith comes from "keeping on keepin' on." Barbara Deming also said it well: "We cannot live without our lives." If we keep silent and let them define the terms of our lives, we have killed ourselves spiritually. I think we get the courage we need by staying with one another. At times we have to be careful what we say, and what we encourage our sisters to say publicly, because the most vitriolic and terrified of our opponents *do* want us dead. They do not want us to name our truths, and we need to be realistic about the times we live in. But we do have to speak when we can. I, for one, intend to live the rest of my life on my own terms, working with my sisters and with men in solidarity with us in the struggle for justice. I will not heed the terms set by men who are intent upon controlling everything in the world. We need to say to these men, "not with our lives, you don't!"

CH: And I would like to say to other women that our solidarity really *is* our survival and that our solidarity does not mean agreement. It does mean cultivating a respect for one another's integrity. By that I mean that where we meet either our own or others' lack of integrity, we say, "That way of dealing with our differences is not acceptable. You can't do this to me or to whomever." This is *not* one of our strengths today, we who are white feminists.

BH: You're right, there's terrible horizontal violence today among white bourgeois women.

CH: What happens, I believe, is that these sisters get captured by the white, liberal male way of thinking. Often they *allow* themselves to be captured. Women *do* have agency, we're not only victims, even if we've been badly hurt. So white women often get themselves caught up in the agenda of men in power, including liberals, and wind up standing more with heterosexist racist patriarchy than with their sisters. We need to call them forth to stand with their sisters. And that's very different than writing them off as hopelessly retrogressive—because, in fact, they are sisters doing what they think they "have" to be doing. They seldom realize how much harm they're inflicting on other women. I believe we need to be about building solidarity, which means hearing criticism about ourselves and learning from it. One thing I try to keep in mind as I teach is that regardless of how inclusive we think we are at any moment of our theological work, we're always leaving someone out. I insist to my students that we need always to be asking, "Who are we leaving out?" or "Who is not here, and why?" and really seek for answers to these important theological and ethical questions.

Another thing I believe in is the erotic character of our created being and in the sacred Spirit as the source of our passion for justice, for right relation with one another, for life, and for God. As I hear it described, even in the attacks upon it, the Re-Imagining conference was a *passionate, erotically empowering* event. I believe we're born into the world to experience and celebrate this—and to struggle for the conditions that will enable us, and all others, to experience and celebrate this passionate, erotic, justice-making Spirit. So I delight in the fact that Re-Imagining happened, and I hope that the participants will take heart in realizing how truly the Spirit was tapped—and called to the larger church's attention—by the conference.

Here I stand enthusiastically with Audre Lorde: We're going to die anyhow, someday, somehow, whether we've spoken or not.[6] So we might as well speak, celebrate, and live on terms that we can work out with the sisters and brothers who stand with us. We don't have to be "right" or "best," but we do have to be clear that we are alive here and now, and that means learning how to hold disagreements in creative tension, not disconnecting from other women simply because their experience is not ours. This takes us back to the question of whether we're going to continue to collude in the spirituality of monopoly capitalism in which there's room for one, and only one, perspective.

BH: You're a good one to give this advice because you bear disagreement with such grace and perspective. Because your theological work is so honest, you've been a recipient of much patronizing contempt from male theologians and, more recently, from other feminists in response to your critique of professionalism and boundaries. Your call for mutual respect is something we all need to hear right now. And you're absolutely right—we have to relate and learn in new ways, not in the arrogant, controlling way we've learned from "experts" who know already whatever needs to be known about other people's lives.

CH: I appreciate what you say. You've certainly seen me through some interesting times and learned a lot with me, haven't you? I want to say that I believe we *all* need to learn how to relate mutually—it's not a lesson we've been taught by the dominant culture or the mainline churches. *You* have tried to embody mutuality with your students for at least twenty-five years. I'm very grateful to you for that and for helping folks understand better than anyone I know the material and spiritual death women face in heterosexist, racist capitalism.

NOTES

CHAPTER 1

Adaptation of sermon at the Episcopal Divinity School in Cambridge, Massachusetts, February 24, 1994.

1. Since each homily, essay, or lecture had a particular audience or congregation, I try to indicate throughout this volume with whom I was identifying as I spoke or wrote—hence, to whom the first-person plural ("we") refers in each case. In this homily, the context is a christian eucharist. I am speaking particularly to christians, trying to help stretch sensibilities about how we might live our faith genuinely in ways that respect and affirm persons of other religious and spiritual traditions.
2. *Boston Globe,* February 6, 1994.
3. Using the lowercase "c" with reference to "christian" is a spiritual, intellectual, and political discipline for me as a member of a religious tradition so arrogant and abusive historically in relation to women, children, and nonruling class men; lesbian/gay/bisexual/transgendered/sexual nonconformists; Jews, Muslims, wicca, and practitioners of other religious traditions; persons whose cultural/racial/ethnic origins are other than European; and all other-than-human members of creation.
4. Blackmun retired from the Court at the end of its 1994 term.
5. *New York Times,* February 23, 1994.
6. Music by Albert Hammond and John Bettis, 1987. Whitney Houston recorded "One Moment in Time" with Arista Records in 1988. The song was used by NBC for their coverage of the 1988 Summer Olympics.
7. Three gold medalists in the 1994 Winter Olympics.
8. See especially Marie M. Fortune, *Is Nothing Sacred?* (San Francisco: Harper and Row, 1989), and Peter Rutter, *Sex in the Forbidden Zone* (New York: St. Martin's Press, 1989). See also Karen Lebacqz and Ronald Barton, *Sex in the Parish* (Louisville: Westminster/John Knox Press, 1991), for a

somewhat less absolutely proscriptive, more nuanced treatment of these issues.

9. See Marie M. Fortune's review of my book, *When Boundaries Betray Us: Beyond Illusions of What Is Ethical in Therapy and Life* (San Francisco: HarperCollins, 1993), in *The Christian Century*, 18–25 May 1994, 524–26, and the exchange between us in *The Christian Century*, 1–8 June 1994, 579–82.

10. Dorothee Sölle, *Revolutionary Patience*, trans. Rita and Robert Kimber (Maryknoll, N.Y.: Orbis Books, 1977).

CHAPTER 2

First published as an editorial in *The Witness* 77, nos. 1 and 2 (January/February 1994): 6.

1. This piece is addressed primarily to progressive christian readers of the only progressive publication associated with the Episcopal church. My assumption here, in this issue devoted entirely to "The Sixties," was that most readers would be interested in "the Sixties" and would remember them (i.e., would be "middle-aged" and older), but that whether or not they had actually lived through this period, most readers would be hoping to make connections between "then" and "now."

CHAPTER 3

An earlier version of this article was first published in *The Christian Century*, 14 March 1990, as one of a series entitled "How My Mind Has Changed."

1. Those with whom I've learned so much about our "we-ness" as the basis of our humanness and creatureliness include primarily my sisterly colleagues in feminist, womanist, and *mujerista* theologies and ethics as well as several feminist psychologists/social theorists/activists who are pushing the boundaries of their own lives and work.

2. Beverly Wildung Harrison, "The Power of Anger in the Work of Love," *Making the Connections: Essays in Feminist Social Ethics*, ed. Carol S. Robb (Boston: Beacon Press, 1985).

3. Judith McDaniel, "The Descent," *Metamorphosis: Reflections on Recovery* (Ithaca, N.Y.: Firebrand Books, 1989), 50–54.

4. I first heard Delores Williams speak of our "lines of continuity" when we were working together with other women as the Mud Flower Collective on *God's Fierce Whimsy: Christian Feminism and Theological Education* (New York: The Pilgrim Press, 1985).

5. In this essay, the "we" I refer to, as in the preceding pieces, is a largely progressive—liberal and liberationist—christian readership, mostly but not entirely white, middle-strata, protestant christians in the United States.

6. See chapter 13 for more on Sophia.

7. See the essay "The Body of Christa" in this volume. "Christa/community" is the christological term employed by Rita Nakashima Brock to designate the praxis of healing and liberation for women who "journey by heart." See Brock's *Journeys by Heart: A Christology of Erotic Power* (New York: Crossroad, 1988). I was introduced to the term "Christa" by English sculptor Edwina Sandys, whose work in bronze by this name was displayed for a few weeks during the mid-1980s in the Cathedral of St. John the Divine in New York City. The public was so agitated by the image of a crucified woman that the Episcopal bishop of New York had the statue removed. I first discussed "Christa" as a redemptive image in *Touching Our Strength: The Erotic as Power and the Love of God* (San Francisco: HarperCollins, 1989).

8. See Delores S. Williams, *Sisters in the Wilderness: The Challenge of Womanist God-Talk* (Maryknoll, N.Y.: Orbis Press, 1993), for attention to the role of Hagar in the African American women's struggles for survival and quality of life in a racist, sexist, and classist society.

9. See Phyllis Trible's treatment of Jephthah's daughter in *Texts of Terror* (Philadelphia: Fortress Press, 1984), 93–116.

10. See Mary Daly, *Gyn/Ecology: The Metaethics of Radical Feminism* (Boston: Beacon Press, 1978).

11. The book in which I first explored our power in mutual relation was *The Redemption of God: A Theology of Mutual Relation* (Lanham, Md.: University Press of America, 1982).

12. I have explored this particular relational rupture and its meanings for me in *When Boundaries Betray Us: Beyond Illusions of What Is Ethical in Therapy and in Life* (San Francisco: HarperCollins, 1993).

13. During the late 1980s and early 1990s numerous essays

and books have been written by christian and post-christian feminists and womanists on the theological, ethical, and pastoral problems with male-oriented understandings of the atonement as the basis of redemptive suffering. See especially Delores Williams, *Sisters in the Wilderness*; Rita Nakashima Brock, *Journeys by Heart*; Joanne Carlson Brown and Carole R. Bohn, eds., *Christianity, Patriarchy, and Abuse* (New York: The Pilgrim Press, 1989); and the theological currents running through my book *When Boundaries Betray Us*. Some of the most important work being done against christian atonement theology is the as-yet unpublished material of Sharon Lewis, a doctoral student at Union Theological Seminary in New York City.

CHAPTER 4

This sermon was given at the ordinations of a gay man and two lesbian women—Jeff Johnson, Ruth Frost, and Phyllis Zillhart—at St. Paulus Lutheran Church, San Francisco, 20 January 1990.

1. See Alice Walker, *The Color Purple* (San Diego: Harcourt Brace Jovanovich, 1982). My citation of Walker at this point raises the important question of when and how it is (and is not) appropriate for white women to draw upon womanist resources (and other resources by women of color) to illustrate something about the experiences of—in this case—an all-white group of women such as the Philadelphia Eleven. I think we women from dominant cultures, races, religions, classes, and other groups need to be aware that we cannot and should not simply "take" and "apply" the lives and contributions of women of color to our own experiences. The fact is, Walker's suggestion in *The Color Purple* about the spiritual experience of Black people—that "[t]hey come to church to *share* God, not find God"—is, historically, a particularly Black church experience which, most decidedly, cannot be applied to the experiences of most Episcopalians. And yet, the Philadelphia ordination, although the ordinands were white, was an event consciously, intentionally, and visibly linked with the struggle for racial as well as gender justice—e.g., the host church (Church of the Advocate in North Philadelphia) had long been led by and primarily

served Black people; many of the leading participants in the service were Black Episcopalians, including the Rev. Paul Washington, rector of the Church of the Advocate; Dr. Charles V. Willie, the highest-ranking layman in the Episcopal Church; and Barbara C. Harris, of the Church of the Advocate, who later would herself be ordained a priest and become the first woman bishop in the Anglican communion. Moreover, most of the ordaining bishops, ordinands, and participants in the service shared strong ongoing commitments to racial, economic, and gender/sexual justice. In this spirit, it was, in fact, a liturgical event which Walker's description truly fits: one in which people came together to share, not find, God. Still, I believe we white women need to think about what and how we "borrow" (Mary E. Hunt's term)—rather than steal—resources from sisters of color. Most of us, certainly I myself, unwittingly and inadvertently have misappropriated resources from especially women of color and Jewish feminists. We need not be defensive or ashamed, but rather we need to keep learning how to meet and learn from others *as they are*, not as we see ourselves in them and not as we may want them to be. See the special section on appropriation, *Journal of Feminist Studies in Religion* 8, no. 2 (fall 1992).

2. The congregation in this service was a largely Lutheran group that included many gay men, lesbians, and others living contrary to traditional christian teachings on sexuality. This sermon was addressed primarily to these gay, lesbian, bisexual, and other "deviant" sisters and brothers—for the most part, but by no means exclusively, white and middle-strata folk.

3. Increasingly, I use the adjective "christic" rather than the noun/name "Christ" with reference to Jesus' power, because it more accurately, I believe, reflects the power of God that moved him as a brother—one among many—rather than as the one and only Son of God. His christic power is ours as well. Christology is an arena of excitement and discovery among feminist and womanist theologians. I am especially grateful to the christological work of Dorothee Sölle, Delores Williams, Rita Nakashima Brock, and Sallie McFague.

CHAPTER 5

Dedicated to Ann Heyward. This sermon was preached at the Commencement Eucharist at the Episcopal Divinity School on 22 May 1991.

1. The congregation in this service was the seminary's 1991 graduating class and their families and friends, largely, but not entirely, a white, middle-strata group of christians, including many Episcopalians, those preparing for ordination, and others.
2. See Sharon Welch, *A Feminist Ethic of Risk* (Minneapolis: Fortress Press, 1990).
3. Beverly Harrison remembers this from Niebuhr's lectures.

CHAPTER 6

Sermon at the ordination of the Reverend Barry Stopfel to the priesthood, Episcopal Church of the Atonement, Tenafly, New Jersey, 14 September 1991. At the time, I did not use the concept of "voices" in the plural. Since then, I have read Ann Kirkus Wetherilt's *That They May Be Many: Voices of Women, Echoes of God* (New York: Continuum, 1994), and am appreciative of her effort to call us away from presenting sacred speech as one uniform or singular "voice" or "word."

1. This, I believe, is what the "malestream" within several protestant denominations, notably the Presbyterian and Methodist churches, realized was the significance of the Re-Imagining conference in Minneapolis in November 1993.
2. This congregation was largely Episcopal, a group of predominantly white, middle-strata men and women, including many gay, lesbian, and bisexual christians.
3. Louie Crew, unpublished.
4. Mariel Kinsey, unpublished.
5. These are some Episcopalians and our friends who have taken public stands either as or on behalf of lesbians and gay men in the church.

CHAPTER 7

Homily at the Episcopal Divinity School, 21 November 1991, in an AIDS healing service.

1. Sam was a friendly Manx who walked with my dogs and me around campus, greeting friends and passersby. He was very much a member of the seminary community and his deteriorating condition had been a matter of shared concern.

CHAPTER 8

Remarks at a candlelight vigil in Boston on 15 October 1993. The gathering of several hundred people was made up largely of white gay men, lesbians, and friends and advocates for gay/lesbian/bisexual/transgendered persons. It seemed to be, for the most part, a fairly secular crowd, not interested in christian spirituality.

CHAPTER 9

Keynote address at National Convention of Parents and Friends of Lesbians and Gays (P-FLAG), Charlotte, North Carolina, 12 October 1991.

1. A year earlier, Harvey Gantt, the Democratic nominee for the U.S. Senate, had been barely beaten in his race against incumbent Jesse Helms.
2. The several hundred person audience was, largely, a white, middle-strata group of women and men in their forties, fifties, and sixties—for the most part, parents and friends of gay, lesbian, and bisexual folks. In making this presentation, I identified myself with the most politically progressive members of the audience.
3. One of the consequences of the white feminist "culture of recovery" (from addiction and abuse) is that drawing from so-called self-help programs as well as psychotherapy, many white women tend to lean on highly individualistic, nuclear-family-based psychological understandings of themselves and their families. There are a number of very positive outcomes of the recovery movement—e.g., awareness of the prevalence of violence against women and children and social movements to eliminate it and creation of support structures for victims of sexual and physical abuse as well as for women struggling with substance-based addictions. See such resources as Ellen Bass and Laura Davis, *The Courage to Heal: A Guide for Women Survivors of Child Sexual Abuse* (New

York: Harper and Row, 1988); Pauline B. Bart and Eileen Geil Moran, eds., *Violence Against Women: The Bloody Footprints* (Newbury Park, Calif.: Sage, 1993); Elisabeth Schüssler Fiorenza and M. Shawn Copeland, eds., "Violence Against Women," *Concilium,* no. 1 (February 1994); Kersti Yllo and Michelle Bograd, eds., *Feminist Perspectives on Wife Abuse* (Newbury Park, Calif.: Sage, 1988).

However, the cultivation of a climate of suspicion toward parents and the correlate memory search for violence in families of origin have created a social climate in which recovering women who express admiration for our parents often are suspected of being out of touch with reality. Too often, as well, because we are social persons shaped psychospiritually by our culture, we begin to suspect ourselves, to wonder if, maybe, the source of a particular pain was, in fact, our father or mother or Uncle Joe or the guy next door. This happened to me, as I discuss in *When Boundaries Betray Us: Beyond Illusions of What Is Ethical in Therapy and Life* (San Francisco: HarperCollins, 1993). When, as in my case, women in recovery from addiction *do* become confused about what happened to us as children, we are summarily dismissed by many feminist therapists as being "in denial," "over-protective" of parents, manifesting "symptoms associated with childhood abuse," when, in fact, our primary struggle was, and is, not with our parents but rather with how the hetero/sexist, classist, racist structures of our lives generated and shaped our childhood pain. See the essay "Alienation and Pastoral Care" in this volume for more on this struggle.

4. The Senate Judiciary Committee hearings on Anita Hill's charges against Clarence Thomas took place during the P-FLAG convention. In the original text, I made several references to this "patriarchal spectacle."

5. Carter Heyward, "Theological Explorations of Homosexuality," *The Witness* 62, no. 6 (June 1979): 13–15, and "Coming Out: Journey Without Maps," *Christianity and Crisis,* 39 (11 June 1979): 153–56.

6. The woman who had organized my visit was Ginny Osborn, a lovely, justice-seeking woman who died tragically several years ago.

7. Anita Bryant, a chief spokesperson against gay men and lesbians, was speaking in Charlotte at the Northside Baptist

Church at the same time I was preaching across town.

8. For resources on the effects of harsh discipline against children, see Alice Miller, *For Your Own Good: Hidden Cruelty in Child-Rearing and the Roots of Violence* (New York: Noonday, 1990); Philip J. Greven, *Spare the Child: The Religious Roots of Punishment and the Psychological Impact of Physical Abuse* (New York: Knopf, 1991).

CHAPTER 10

This is adapted from the text of a Bennett-Morton Lecture, an annual event established at the Claremont School of Theology, Claremont, California, in memory of Anne McGrew Bennett and Nelle Morton, prominent religious activists in the struggles for justice, including feminism. The lecture was given on 22 March 1994. The audience was largely students, faculty, and friends of Claremont and of Nelle Morton and Anne Bennett. It was a politically and theologically progressive gathering, mainly white, middle strata, highly educated, and protestant christian. An earlier, more "secular" version of the paper was presented on 30 April 1993, at the "Learning from Women Conference" in Boston, sponsored by the Harvard Medical School, the Cambridge Hospital, and the Stone Center of Wellesley College. The earlier paper was entitled, "Forces That Silence, Separate, and Shatter Us: Is There a Chance for the Future?"

1. This section on alienation is adapted from my book *Touching Our Strength: The Erotic as Power and the Love of God* (San Francisco: Harper and Row, 1989), 48–60.

2. See Paul Tillich, *Systematic Theology*, 3 vols. (Chicago: University of Chicago Press, 1951–63).

3. See Bertell Ollmann, *Alienation: Marx's Conception of Man in Capitalist Society* (New York: Cambridge University Press, 1976), and several early resources by Karl Marx in Robert C. Tucker, ed., *The Marx-Engels Reader* (New York: W. W. Norton, 1978), 26–52, 66–132; see also Erich Fromm, *Marx's Concept of Man* (New York: Ungar, 1969).

4. See Jean Baker Miller, "Connections, Disconnections, and Violations," unpublished, Stone Center, Wellesley, Mass., 1988), 7.

5. See Carol Gilligan and Ann Rogers, *Women, Girls, and Psycho-*

therapy: Reframing Resistance (New York: Haworth Press, 1991).

6. See Carter Heyward, *Touching Our Strength: The Erotic as Power and the Love of God* (San Francisco: Harper and Row, 1989).

7. On class, see Barbara Ehrenreich, *Fear of Falling: The Inner Life of the Middle Class* (New York: HarperCollins, 1990); Lillian Breslin Rubin, *Worlds of Pain* (New York: Basic Books, 1976); Manning Marable, *The Crisis of Color and Democracy: Essays on Race, Class, and Power* (Monroe, Me.: Common Courage Press, 1992); Michael Harrington, *The Other America: Poverty in the United States* (Baltimore: Penguin, 1963); Richard Sennett and Jonathan Cobb, *The Hidden Injuries of Class* (New York: W. W. Norton, 1972).

8. See Barth's *The Epistle to the Romans* (New York: Oxford University Press, 1968), 48–54. For further discussion of the concept, see the later volumes of Barth's *Church Dogmatics* (Edinburgh: T. and T. Clark, 1936–69).

9. See Delores S. Williams, *Sisters in the Wilderness: The Challenge of Womanist God-Talk* (Maryknoll, N.Y.: Orbis Press, 1993).

10. Audre Lorde, *Sister Outsider: Essays and Speeches* (Trumansburg, N.Y.: Crossing Press, 1984), 161–62.

11. See M. Brinton Lykes, "The Caring Self: Social Experiences of Power and Powerlessness," *Who Cares? Theory, Research, and Educational Implications of the Ethic of Care,* ed. Mary Brabeck (New York: Praeger, 1989); see also "Gender and Individualistic Versus Collectivist Bases for Notions About the Self," *Journal of Personality* 53, no. 2 (1985).

12. See Judith V. Jordan, Alexandra Kaplan, Jean Baker Miller, Irene P. Stiver, and Janet L. Surrey, *Women's Growth in Connection: Writings from the Stone Center* (New York: Guilford Press, 1991).

13. See Martin Buber, *I and Thou* (New York: Charles Scribner's Sons, 1970).

14. See Thich Nhat Hahn's, *Touching Peace: Practicing the Art of Mindful Living* (Berkeley, Calif.: Parallax Press, 1992); *The Heart of Understanding: Commentaries on the Prajnaparamita Heart Sutra* (Berkeley, Calif.: Parallax Press, 1988); and *The Sun My Heart: From Mindfulness to Insight Contemplation* (Berkeley, Calif.: Parallax Press, 1988).

15. This is a basic tenet of feminist liberation theology and is addressed, increasingly, by almost all feminist, womanist, and *mujerista* theologians. See, for example, the Mud Flower Collective, *God's Fierce Whimsy: Christian Feminism and Theological Education* (New York: The Pilgrim Press, 1985); Susan Brooks Thistlethwaite and Mary Engel Potter, eds., *Lift Every Voice: Theology from the Underside* (San Francisco: Harper and Row, 1990); Susan Brooks Thistlethwaite, *Sex, Race, and God* (New York: Crossroad, 1989); Ada Maria Isasi-Diaz, *En la Lucha: A Hispanic Women's Liberation Theology* (Minneapolis: Fortress Press, 1993); bell hooks, *Yearning: Race, Gender, and Cultural Politics* (Boston: South End Press, 1990); Audre Lorde, *Sister Outsider: Essays and Speeches* (Trumansburg, N.Y.: Crossing Press, 1984), 114–23; Joan M. Martin, "The Notion of Difference, For Emerging Womanist Ethics: The Writings of Audre Lorde and bell hooks," *Journal of Feminist Studies in Religion* 9, nos. 1–2 (1993): 39–51; Sharon Welch, *Communities of Solidarity and Resistance* (Maryknoll, N.Y.: Orbis Press, 1985).

16. Nelle Morton, *The Journey Is Home* (Boston: Beacon, 1985).

17. Some of the most important resources for survivors of childhood sexual abuse include Judith Lewis Herman, *Trauma and Recovery: The Aftermath of Violence—From Domestic Abuse to Political Terror* (New York: Basic Books, 1992); Judith Lewis Herman, *Father-Daughter Incest* (Cambridge, Mass.: Harvard University Press, 1981); Ellen Bass and Laura Davis, *The Courage to Heal* (New York: Harper and Row, 1988), and Laura Davis, *The Courage to Heal Workbook* (New York: Harper and Row, 1988); Alice Miller, *Thou Shalt Not Be Aware: Society's Betrayal of the Child* (New York: Farrar, Straus, and Giroux, 1984), and Alice Miller, *The Untouched Key: Tracing Childhood Trauma in Creativity and Destructiveness* (New York: Doubleday, 1990).

18. Personal correspondence, 1993.

19. Personal correspondence, 1993.

20. See my sermon, "Not Knowing for Sure: On Humility," the exchange between Marie M. Fortune and me in *The Christian Century*, "Boundaries or Barriers?" 1–8 June 1994, 579–82, and Fortune's review of my book in *The Christian Century*, "Therapy and Intimacy: Confused About Boundaries," 18–25 May 1994, 524–26.

21. See Donna J. Haraway, *Simians, Cyborgs, and Women: The Reinvention of Nature* (New York: Routledge, 1991), 187.
22. Frederick Denison Maurice taught that you can't teach a child obedience and hope that he or she will be able to develop a conscience. See F. D. Maurice, *The Conscience: Lectures on Casuistry* (London: Macmillan, 1883). I agree, and I believe that adults cannot simultaneously simply obey rules and struggle honestly with serious ethical questions the rules are intended to govern.
23. See Nelle Morton, *The Journey Is Home* (Boston: Beacon Press, 1985).

CHAPTER 11

A version of this piece appeared originally as "The Bear and Bosnia" in *The Witness* 76, no. 10 (October 1993): 8–11 (1249 Washington Boulevard, Ste. 3115, Detroit, Mich. 48226–1822). The readership of the magazine is predominantly white, progressive—liberal and radical—protestant christian (Episcopal).

1. Paul H. Santmire, *The Travail of Nature: The Ambiguous Ecological Promise of Christian Theology* (Philadelphia: Fortress Press, 1985).
2. Ibid., 217.
3. Compare Rosemary Radford Ruether, *Gaia and God: An Ecofeminist Theology* (San Francisco: HarperCollins, 1992); Sallie McFague, *The Body of God: An Ecological Theology* (Minneapolis: Augsburg Fortress Press, 1993); J. Michael Clark, *Beyond Our Ghettoes: Gay Theology in Ecological Perspective* (Cleveland: The Pilgrim Press, 1993); and Daniel Teberg Spencer, "Christian Ethics, 'Gay and Gaia': A Liberationist Contribution to Christian Ecological Ethics" (Ph.D. dissertation, Union Theological Seminary, 1994).
4. For more on transcendence, see Tom F. Driver's work, including *Patterns of Grace: Human Experience as Word of God* (San Francisco: Harper and Row, 1977); *Christ in a Changing World: Toward an Ethical Christology* (New York: Crossroad Press, 1981); and *The Magic of Ritual* (San Francisco: HarperCollins, 1991). See also my short essay "Crossing Over: On Transcendence," in *Our Passion for Justice: Images of Power, Sexuality, and Liberation* (New York: The Pilgrim Press, 1984), 243–47.

5. I appreciate especially Delores S. Williams's insight that "quality of life"—in particular, for African American women—is a foundation and goal of right relation. In relation to animals, as well as for people, I would suggest that "quality of life" (kindness as well as food, shelter/humane environment, and health care) at times supersedes merely physical "survival" as the basis for sustaining right, mutual, relation. A similar point is made by ethicists such as Beverly W. Harrison, Mary E. Hunt, Christine Gudorf, Frances Kissling, and others involved in the struggle for women's reproductive freedom, including safe, legal abortion provisions. See especially Beverly Wildung Harrison, *Our Right to Choose: Toward an Ethic of Abortion* (Boston: Beacon Press, 1983); Rosalind Pollack Petchesky, *Abortion and Woman's Choice: The State, Sexuality, and Reproductive Freedom* (Boston: Northeastern University Press, 1990).

6. Chung Hyun Kyung, "Come, Holy Spirit, Renew the Whole Creation," *Signs of the Spirit*, report of the Seventh Assembly, World Council of Churches, Geneva, Switzerland, 1991.

7. Ursula LeGuin, *Buffalo Gals and Other Animal Presences* (New York: Penguin/New American Library, 1987), 11.

CHAPTER 12

Adapted from a presentation at Sexuality and the Integrity of Relationships Conference, Episcopal Divinity School, Cambridge, Massachusetts, February 4–5, 1994.

1. In particular I am identifying in this piece with women and men who are actively struggling to know more honestly what our bodies can teach us about sex and God. The audience on this occasion was mostly white, middle-strata, highly educated Episcopalians. In fact, I assumed that those most likely to "hear" me would be those most open—personally and professionally and politically—to stretching beyond most of the prevailing assumptions, among white christian feminists as well as other christians, about sexual identity and sexual ethics.

2. This talk was given in tandem with a presentation by Renee Hill, African American priest, lesbian, and womanist theologian.

3. See *The Redemption of God: A Theology of Mutual Relation*

(Lanham, Md.: University Press of America, 1982) for more on verb "to god."

4. See the concluding piece in this volume, a response to the reaction against the Re-Imagining conference (Minneapolis, November 1993), for more about the backlash against spirited women. Anne E. Gilson's new book celebrates the erotic power of many lesbians and others through whom "eros is breaking free." See her *Eros Breaking Free: Interpreting Sexual Theo-Ethics* (Cleveland: The Pilgrim Press, 1995).

CHAPTER 13

Adaptation of an address at Anglican Women's Encounter in Salvador, Bahia, Brazil, 3 April 1992. The original presentation was published in *No North or South: Worldwide Anglican Encounter,* ed. Claire Woodley-Aitchison (New York: Episcopal Church Center [815 Second Avenue, New York, N.Y. 10017], 1993).

1. From an earlier address by Chung Hyun Kyung.
2. Thich Nhat Hahn, *The Heart of Understanding: Commentaries on the Prajnaparamita Heart Sutra* (Berkeley, Calif.: Parallax Press, 1988).

CHAPTER 14

1. Ruth Nicastro, *Journal of Women's Ministries,* Official Publication of the Council for Women's Ministries of the Episcopal Church, vol. 10, no. 1 (spring 1994): 14.
2. Morrison was issuing this call on behalf of CLOUT— Christian Lesbians Out Together.
3. This presentation, "Body of Christa: Hope of the World," is included in this book.
4. As several of the pieces in this volume have indicated, eleven women were ordained priests in a service in Philadelphia on 29 July 1974, prior to the Episcopal Church's authorization of the ordination of women priests. The official response from the bishops of the church was to declare our ordinations "invalid"—that is, to erase them entirely as if nothing had happened. We eleven priests and many thousands of other Episcopalians refused to accept the bishops' ruling. A year later, in Washington, D.C., four more women were or-

dained "irregularly," and in the fall of 1976 the Episcopal Church approved the ordination of women priests. Although they never retracted their judgment that our ordinations were null and void, we were allowed to be "regularized" in services in which our bishops welcomed us back into good standing in the Episcopal Church—as priests.

5. *When Boundaries Betray Us: Beyond Illusions of What Is Ethical in Therapy and in Life* (San Francisco: HarperCollins, 1993).

6. See Audre Lorde, "The Transformation of Silence into Language and Action," *Sister Outsider: Essays and Speeches* (Trumansburg, N.Y.: Crossing, 1984).

BIBLIOGRAPHY

Barrington, Judith, ed. *An Intimate Wilderness: Lesbian Writers on Sexuality*. Portland, Ore.: Eighth Mountain Press, 1991.

Bart, Pauline B., and Moran, Eileen Geil, eds. *Violence Against Women: The Bloody Footprints*. Newbury Park, Calif.: Sage, 1993.

Barth, Karl. *The Epistle to the Romans*. New York: Oxford University Press, 1968.

———. *Church Dogmatics*. Edinburgh: T. and T. Clark, 1936–69.

Bass, Ellen, and Laura Davis. *The Courage to Heal: A Guide for Women Survivors of Child Sexual Abuse*. New York: Harper and Row, 1988.

Batstone, David, ed. *New Visions for the Americas: Religious Engagement and Social Transformation*. Minneapolis: Fortress Press, 1993.

Bozarth, Alla Renée. *Lifelines: Threads of Grace Through Seasons of Change*. Kansas City, Mo.: Sheed and Ward, 1994.

Brock, Rita Nakashima. *Journeys by Heart: A Christology of Erotic Power*. New York: Crossroad, 1988.

Brown, Joanne Carlson, and Carole R. Bohn, eds. *Christianity, Patriarchy, and Abuse*. New York: Pilgrim Press, 1989.

Buber, Martin. *I and Thou*. New York: Charles Scribner's Sons, 1970.

Chung Hyun Kyung. *Struggle to Be the Sun Again: Introducing Asian Women's Theology*. Maryknoll, N.Y.: Orbis, 1990.

———. "Come, Holy Spirit, Renew the Whole Creation," *Signs of the Spirit*, report of the Seventh Assembly, World Council of Churches, Geneva, Switzerland, 1991.

Clark, J. Michael. *Beyond Our Ghettoes: Gay Theology in Ecological Perspective*. Cleveland: Pilgrim Press, 1993.

Clark, J. Michael, and Michael L. Stemmler, eds. *Spirituality and Community: Diversity in Lesbian and Gay Experience*. Las Colinas, Tex.: Monument, 1994.

Daly, Mary. *Gyn/Ecology: The Metaethics of Radical Feminism*. Boston: Beacon Press, 1978.

Davies, Susan E., and Eleanor H. Haney, eds. *Redefining Sexual*

Ethics: A Sourcebook of Essays, Stories, and Poems. Cleveland: The Pilgrim Press, 1991.

Davis, Laura. *The Courage to Heal Workbook.* New York: Harper and Row, 1988.

Driver, Tom F. *Patterns of Grace: Human Experience as Word of God.* San Francisco: Harper and Row, 1977.

————. *Christ in a Changing World: Toward an Ethical Christology.* New York: Crossroad Press, 1981.

————. *The Magic of Ritual.* San Francisco: HarperCollins, 1991.

Ehrenreich, Barbara, *Fear of Falling: The Inner Life of the Middle Class.* New York: HarperCollins, 1990.

Fabella, Virginia, and Mercy Amba Oduyoye, eds. *With Passion and Compassion: Third World Women Doing Theology.* Maryknoll, N.Y.: Orbis, 1988.

Felder, Richard E., and Avrum Geurin Weiss. *Experiential Psychotherapy: A Symphony of Selves.* Lanham, Md.: University Press of America, 1991.

Fiorenza, Elisabeth Schüssler, and Copeland, M. Shawn, eds., "Violence Against Women," *Concilium,* no. 1, February 1994.

Fortune, Marie M. *Is Nothing Sacred?* San Francisco: Harper and Row, 1989.

Fromm, Erich. *Marx's Concept of Man.* New York: Ungar, 1969.

Gilligan, Carol, and Rogers, Ann. *Women, Girls, and Psychotherapy: Reframing Resistance.* New York: Haworth Press, 1991.

Gilson, Anne E. *Eros Breaking Free: Interpreting Sexual Theo-Ethics.* Cleveland: The Pilgrim Press, 1995.

Greenspan, Miriam. *A New Approach to Women and Therapy.* 10th anniversary edition with a new introduction. Blue Ridge Summit, Pa.: Tab Books, 1993.

Greven, Philip J. *Spare the Child: The Religious Roots of Punishment and the Psychological Impact of Physical Abuse.* New York: Knopf, 1991.

Grey, Mary. *Feminism, Redemption, and the Christian Tradition.* Mystic, Conn.: Twenty-Third Publications, 1990.

Hagan, Kay Leigh. *Women Respond to the Men's Movement.* San Francisco: Pandora (Harper), 1992.

Hahn, Thich Nhat. *The Heart of Understanding: Commentaries on the Prajnaparamita Heart Sutra.* Berkeley, Calif.: Parallax Press, 1988.

————. *The Sun My Heart: From Mindfulness to Insight Contemplation.* Berkeley, Calif.: Parallax Press, 1988.

————. *Touching Peace: Practicing the Art of Mindful Living.* Berkeley, Calif.: Parallax Press, 1992.

Haraway, Donna J. *Simians, Cyborgs, and Women: The Reinvention of Nature.* New York: Routledge, 1991.

Harrington, Michael. *The Other America: Poverty in the United States.* Baltimore: Penguin, 1963.

Harrison, Beverly Wildung. *Our Right to Choose: Toward an Ethic of Abortion.* Boston: Beacon Press, 1983.

————. "The Power of Anger in the Work of Love," *Making the Connections: Essays in Feminist Social Ethics.* Edited by Carol S. Robb. Boston: Beacon Press, 1985.

Herman, Judith Lewis. *Trauma and Recovery: The Aftermath of Violence—From Domestic Abuse to Political Terror.* New York: Basic Books, 1992.

————. *Father-Daughter Incest.* Cambridge, Mass.: Harvard University Press, 1981.

Heyward, Carter, "Theological Explorations of Homosexuality," *The Witness* 62, no. 6, June 1979.

————. "Coming Out: Journey Without Maps," *Christianity and Crisis,* 39, June 11, 1979.

————. *The Redemption of God: A Theology of Mutual Relation.* Lanham, Md.: University Press of America, 1982.

————. "Crossing Over: On Transcendence," *Our Passion for Justice: Images of Power, Sexuality, and Liberation.* New York: Pilgrim Press, 1984.

————. *Touching Our Strength: The Erotic as Power and the Love of God.* San Francisco: HarperCollins, 1989.

————. *When Boundaries Betray Us: Beyond Illusions of What Is Ethical in Therapy and Life.* San Francisco: HarperCollins, 1993.

hooks, bell. *Yearning: Race, Gender, and Cultural Politics.* Boston: South End Press, 1990.

Isasi-Diaz, Ada Maria. *En la Lucha: A Hispanic Women's Liberation Theology.* Minneapolis: Fortress Press, 1993.

Jordan, Judith V., Alexandra Kaplan, Jean Baker Miller, Irene P. Stiver, and Janet L. Surrey. *Women's Growth in Connection: Writings from the Stone Center.* New York: Guilford Press, 1991.

Laidlaw, Toni Ann, Cheryl Malmo, and associates. *Healing*

Voices: Feminist Approaches to Therapy with Women. San Francisco: Jossey-Bass, 1990.

Lebacqz, Karen, and Ronald Barton. *Sex in the Parish.* Louisville: Westminster/John Knox Press, 1991.

LeGuin, Ursula. *Buffalo Gals and Other Animal Presences.* New York: Penguin/New American Library, 1987.

Lorde, Audre. *Sister Outsider: Essays and Speeches.* Trumansburg, N.Y.: Crossing Press, 1984.

Lykes, M. Brinton. "The Caring Self: Social Experiences of Power and Powerlessness." In *Who Cares? Theory, Research, and Educational Implications of the Ethic of Care,* edited by Mary Brabeck. New York: Praeger, 1989.

Macy, Joanna. *World as Lover, World as Self.* Berkeley, Calif.: Parallax, 1991.

McDaniel, Judith. "The Descent." In *Metamorphosis: Reflections on Recovery.* Ithaca: Firebrand Books, 1989.

McFague, Sallie. *The Body of God: An Ecological Theology.* Minneapolis: Augsburg/Fortress Press, 1993.

Marable, Manning. *The Crisis of Color and Democracy: Essays on Race, Class and Power.* Monroe, Me.: Common Courage Press, 1992.

Martin, Joan M. "The Notion of Difference, for Emerging Womanist Ethics: The Writings of Audre Lorde and bell hooks." *Journal of Feminist Studies in Religion* 9, nos. 1–2, 1993.

Maurice, Frederick Denison. *The Conscience: Lectures on Casuistry.* London: Macmillan, 1883.

Miller, Alice. *Thou Shalt Not Be Aware: Society's Betrayal of the Child.* New York: Farrar, Straus, Giroux, 1984.

———. *For Your Own Good: Hidden Cruelty in Child-Rearing and the Roots of Violence.* New York: Noonday, 1990.

———. *The Untouched Key: Tracing Childhood Trauma in Creativity and Destructiveness.* New York: Doubleday, 1990.

Morton, Nelle. *The Journey Is Home.* Boston: Beacon, 1985.

Mud Flower Collective. *God's Fierce Whimsy: Christian Feminism and Theological Education.* New York: The Pilgrim Press, 1985.

Nelson, James B., and Sandra P. Longfellow, eds. *Sexuality and the Sacred: Sources for Theological Reflection.* Louisville: Westminster/John Knox, 1994.

Nicastro, Ruth. *Journal of Women's Ministries.* Official Publication of the Council for Women's Ministries of the Episcopal

Church, vol. 10, no. 1, spring 1994.

Ollmann, Bertell. *Alienation: Marx's Conception of Man in Capitalist Society.* New York: Cambridge University Press, 1976.

Petchesky, Rosalind Pollack. *Abortion and Woman's Choice: The State, Sexuality, and Reproductive Freedom.* Boston: Northeastern University Press, 1990.

Procter-Smith, Marjorie, and Janet R. Walton, eds. *Women at Worship: Interpretations of North American Diversity.* Louisville: Westminster/John Knox, 1993.

Rasmussen, Larry L. *Moral Fragments and Moral Community: A Proposal for Church in Society.* Minneapolis: Fortress, 1993.

Rubin, Lillian Breslin. *Worlds of Pain.* New York: Basic Books, 1976.

Ruether, Rosemary Radford. *Gaia and God: An Ecofeminist Theology.* San Francisco: HarperCollins, 1992.

Rutter, Peter. *Sex in the Forbidden Zone: When Men in Power Betray Women's Trust.* New York: St. Martin's Press, 1989.

Santmire, Paul H. *The Travail of Nature: The Ambiguous Ecological Promise of Christian Theology.* Philadelphia: Fortress Press, 1985.

Sennett, Richard, and Jonathan Cobb. *The Hidden Injuries of Class.* New York: W. W. Norton, 1972.

Sölle, Dorothee. *Revolutionary Patience.* Translated by Rita and Robert Kimber. Maryknoll, N.Y.: Orbis Books, 1977.

Sölle, Dorothee, with Shirley A. Cloyes. *To Work and to Love: A Theology of Creation.* Philadelphia: Fortress, 1984.

Spencer, Daniel Teberg. "Christian Ethics, 'Gay and Gaia': A Liberationist Contribution to Christian Ecological Ethics." Ph.D. dissertation, Union Theological Seminary, 1994.

Starhawk. *Truth or Dare: Encounters with Power, Authority, and Mystery.* San Francisco: Harper and Row, 1987.

Thistlethwaite, Susan Brooks. *Sex, Race, and God.* New York: Crossroad, 1989.

Thistlethwaite, Susan Brooks, and Mary Engel Potter, eds. *Lift Every Voice: Theology from the Underside.* San Francisco: Harper and Row, 1990.

Thompsett, Fredrica Harris. *Courageous Incarnation: In Intimacy, Work, Childhood, and Aging.* Cambridge/Boston: Cowley, 1993.

Tillich, Paul. *Systematic Theology.* 3 vols. Chicago: University of Chicago Press, 1951–63.

Trible, Phyllis. *Texts of Terror.* Philadelphia: Fortress Press, 1984.

Tucker, Robert C., ed. *The Marx-Engels Reader*. New York: W. W. Norton, 1978.

Walker, Alice. *The Color Purple*. San Diego: Harcourt Brace Jovanovich, 1982.

Weeks, Jeffrey. *Against Nature: Essays on History, Sexuality, and Identity*. London: Rivers Oram Press, 1991.

Wetherilt, Ann Kirkus. *That They May Be Many: Voices of Women, Echoes of God*. New York: Continuum, 1994.

Welch, Sharon. *Communities of Solidarity and Resistance*. Maryknoll, N.Y.: Orbis Press, 1985.

————. *A Feminist Ethic of Risk*. Minneapolis: Fortress Press, 1990.

Williams, Delores S. *Sisters in the Wilderness: The Challenge of Womanist God-Talk*. Maryknoll, N.Y.: Orbis Press, 1993.

Wondra, Ellen K. *Humanity Has Been a Holy Thing: Toward a Contemporary Feminist Christology*. Lanham, Md.: University Press of America, 1994.

Woodley-Aitchison, Claire, ed. *No North or South: Worldwide Anglican Encounter*. New York: Episcopal Church Center (815 Second Avenue, New York, N.Y. 10017), 1993.

Yllo, Kersti, and Michelle Bograd, eds. *Feminist Perspectives on Wife Abuse*. Newbury Park, Calif.: Sage, 1988.

INDEX

abortion, 11
AIDS, 33, 35, 52, 59, 62, 67, 69
alcoholism, 21
alienation, 79–98, 139
animals, as sacred others, 102,
    105–11
arrogance: in mainstream religion,
    139, 146; in relation to humility,
    6–8, 10; as root of exploitation, 9
atonement, 136–37
Augustine, 80, 117

Baker Miller, Jean, 81
Barrett, Ellen, 58
Barth, Karl, 83–84
Bennett, Anne, 77
Bennett, John, 77
Blackmun, Harry, 3–6, 8, 11
black theology, 15
boundaries, 48, 149–50; defined,
    108
Brown, Bob, 77
Browning, Ed, 125, 128
Buber, Martin, 16, 88
Byham, Kim, 58

capitalism, 56; global, 14, 22–23,
    138; spirituality of, 137–38, 149
Carl, Elizabeth, 58
Christa, 110; body of, 123–25; as
    community, 22; as participation,
    129–31; as reformation, 133; as
    sacrament, 125–28
christian: use of small 'c,' 151; voca-
    tion, 3, 5–6, 9, 14, 34, 43, 50,
    60, 102, 120, 128
christic, 36; defined, 156

Chung Hyun Kyung, 109, 135,
    136, 138
church(es), 41–42, 54–56, 60, 64,
    69–70, 140, 146; abusive tradi-
    tions of, 96; Anglican/ Epis-
    copal, 124–33; eco-friendly tra-
    ditions in, 102; responsibility of,
    109; on sexuality, 112–20; on
    syncretism, 109; traditions of
    domination in, 102–5
Clark, J. Michael, 103
classism, 51, 78, 83, 90, 93–95
co-inherence, doctrine of, 61–62
coming out, 31–38, 50, 112–13,
    143–46
compassion, 33, 57, 61–62, 64–65,
    91, 95, 120, 125, 129–30
Cone, James, 77
Corrigan, Daniel, 29–30
Crew, Louie, 52, 58
Croneberger, Jack and Marilyn, 58

Daly, Mary, 23
death penalty, 11
Deming, Barbara, 147
DeWitt, Robert, 49–50
Driver, Tom, 117

election, doctrine of, 60–61
embodiment, 116, 118, 143
epistemology, 116, 118, 137–38

feminist liberation theology, 15,
    104–5, 109–10, 119–20
Francis of Assisi, 103, 105

Gantt, Harvey, 66
Gilligan, Carol, 81

173

CARTER HEYWARD is professor of theology at
Episcopal Divinity School, Cambridge, Massachusetts.

Other Carter Heyward titles from The Pilgrim Press:

OUR PASSION FOR JUSTICE
Images of Power, Sexuality, and Liberation
Powerfully addresses the issues of racism, sexism, exploitation, and oppression from a feminist standpoint, insisting
that the appropriate position for Christians is always on the
side of justice.

Paperback/ISBN 0-8298-0705-5

SPEAKING OF CHRIST
A Lesbian Feminist Voice
The uncompromising writings of one of present-day Christianity's most original thinkers, inviting us to respond faithfully and radically by taking the risks necessary to secure
genuine justice in society.

Paperback/ISBN 0-8298-0829-9